100 FACTS

Nottingham Forest

Steve Horton

Bedford, England

First published in Great Britain in 2020
by Wymer Publishing
www.wymerpublishing.co.uk
Wymer Publishing is a trading name of Wymer (UK) Ltd

First edition. Copyright © 2020 Steve Horton / Wymer Publishing.

ISBN: 978-1-912782-46-8

Edited by Jerry Bloom.

The Author hereby asserts his rights to be identified
as the author of this work in accordance with sections
77 to 78 of the Copyright, Designs & Patents Act 1988.

All rights reserved. No part of this publication may be
reproduced or transmitted in any form or by any means,
electronic or mechanical, including photocopying, or any
information storage and retrieval system, without written
permission from the publisher.

This publication is sold subject to the condition that it shall not,
by way of trade or otherwise, be lent, re-sold, hired out or
otherwise circulated without the publishers prior consent in any
form of binding or cover other than that in which it is published
and without a similar condition including this condition
being imposed on the subsequent purchaser.

Typeset and Design by Andy Bishop / 1016 Sarpsborg
Printed by CMP, Poole, Dorset

A catalogue record for this book is available from the British Library.

Sketches by Becky Welton. © 2014.

100 FACTS

Nottingham Forest

FACT 1
1865 NOTTINGHAM FOREST

Nottingham Forest were formed in 1865 by a shinty team that opted to change the sport they played.

The players attended a special meeting at the Clinton Arms hotel in Shakespeare Street. This was to discuss a proposal by J. S. Scrimshaw that they played football instead of shinty, a game similar to hockey. Members agreed and also purchased twelve red caps, which became the club colours.

The founder members were A Barks, W Brown, W P Brown, C F Daft, T Gamble, R P Hawkesley, T G Howitt, W I Hussey, W R Lymberry, J Milford, J H Rastall, W H Revis, J G Richardson, J S Scrimshaw and J Tomlinson.

The name Nottingham Forest derives from what is now called the Forest Recreation Ground, where early fixtures were played. This was the southernmost part of Sherwood Forest and became protected by legislation in 1845 that restricted it to recreational use only.

There was a period of transition and it was not until March 1866 that Nottingham Forest Football Club played its first game against Notts County.

FACT 2

1866
THE
FIRST DERBY

Arguably the oldest derby rivalry in word football, Nottingham Forest met their near neighbours Notts County for the first time in 1866.

The game was played at the Forest Recreation Ground on 22nd March. It was billed as the red-shirted Garibaldis of Forest versus the maroon and mustard-striped Lambs of Notts County and finished in a 0-0 draw.

Nowadays the two clubs stadiums are separated by the River Trent and just 400 metres apart, making it the closest rivalry in English football. Due to the clubs playing at different levels, they have not met as often as could be expected and the vast majority of Forest fans see Derby as their main rivals.

Whichever way it is looked at, Forest has the best head to head record. In the league, the clubs have met 86 times, with Forest winning 35 of them to County's 28. Forest won three of the five FA Cup ties between the clubs as well as the two occasions they have met in the League Cup.

Forest's biggest winning margin in the fixture is 5-0, which occurred at the City Ground in 1900 and 1953. At County's Meadow Lane ground, they won 6-2 in 1932 and 4-0 in 1991.

1874
SAMUEL WIDDOWSON'S SHINGUARDS

FACT 3

Shinpads, as they are now commonly known, were used for the first time in football in 1874 by a Nottingham Forest player. He was ridiculed at the time but they became widely used.

Born in 1851, Sam Widdowson was an all-round sportsman who also played cricket for Nottinghamshire. He was a fine sprinter who could run 100 yards in just 10.25 seconds.

Frustrated by players getting injured unnecessarily, in 1874 Widdowson cut down a pair of cricket pads and strapped them to the outside of his socks. He was mocked by opponents, but players soon saw their safety value. A local company began producing and marketing ready-made pairs to be worn inside socks.

As captain of Forest, he divided the playing system of two full backs, two half backs and five forwards. This 2-3-5 formation became the basis of the game in England until the 1960s.

After retiring Widdowson was a notable football administrator. As Forest chairman he represented the club at a meeting of the Football League in 1888, where he failed to gain their election. Widdowson remained living in Nottingham all his life and died in 1927.

FACT 4

1879
INTO
THE FA CUP

Nottingham Forest entered the FA Cup for the first time in 1879-80 and almost went all the way to the final.

In the first round Forest were paired at home with neighbours Notts County. At Trent Bridge on 8th November County had the better of the early play, but one of their players had to go off injured. Forest took advantage and ran out 4-0 winners.

Forest won 6-0 at Lancashire club Turton in the second round and faced opposition from that same county in the third. Again they won 6-0, this time against Blackburn Rovers at Trent Bridge.

The fourth round tie with Sheffield at Trent Bridge ended in a thrilling 2-2 draw. The opposition refused to play extra time, believing a replay in Sheffield was more appropriate. The rules stated that extra time could be played if one side requested it and Sheffield were disqualified.

Forest then received a bye to the semi-final due to an odd number of teams being left in the competition. It was there that the marvellous run finally came to an end when they were beaten 1-0 by Oxford University at The Oval.

FACT 5

1883
LEAVING
TRENT BRIDGE

Nottingham Forest found themselves homeless prior to the start of the 1883-84 season and had to move out to Lenton to play their home fixtures.

Since their formation, Forest had played home games at the Forest Recreation Ground, The Meadows and Trent Bridge. For three seasons they had been hiring Trent Bridge, which was by far the best venue in Nottingham, from the county cricket club.

During the summer of 1883, Notts County appointed a new secretary, Edwin Browne, who was also employed by the cricket club. It didn't take Forest officials long to realise that County were more likely to be offered a lease at Trent Bridge for the forthcoming season.

Forest's options were limited and they opted for a field off Derby Road in Lenton, which they named Parkside. The pitch was uneven and sloped, but it was the best they could do. The first game was on 22nd September against Small Heath, which Forest won 3-2 in front of 3,000 spectators.

Although Forest attracted decent sized crowds against top class opposition, most attendances were below 1,000. In December 1884 a match against Small Heath on a rainy December afternoon attracted only 150. At the end of that season the club decided it was time to move again.

FACT 6
1885
FA CUP SEMI-FINAL
IN SCOTLAND

Nottingham Forest reached the semi-final of the FA Cup in 1884-85. After drawing the first game with Queens Park in Derby, they had to travel to Edinburgh for the replay.

Scottish clubs were allowed to play in England's premier cup competition until 1886. Queens Park were Scotland's leading club, having won their own cup competition four years running and losing the English final in 1884.

In the quarter final Forest won 2-0 at Old Etonians, twice winners of the FA Cup. They were then drawn against Queens Park in the semi-final with Derby Cricket Ground being named as the venue. Forest led 1-0 at half time but a late Queens Park equaliser meant a replay was necessary.

Queens appealed for this to take place in Scotland and the FA agreed, with a cricket field at Merchiston Castle school hosting the game on 28th March. A temporary grandstand was constructed and the crowd of 15,000 was the largest to witness a sporting event in the Scottish capital.

Four special excursion trains carried fans north, but they were to return home disappointed. On a dull and windy day Forest's performance matched the weather and they were beaten 3-0. This remains the only time an FA Cup semi-final has been played outside England.

FACT 7

1885
THE
GREGORY GROUND

When Nottingham Forest left Parkside they did not go far, moving to the Gregory Ground that was used by Lenton Cricket Club.

Forest only took about a month making the ground suitable for football crowds. They erected two wooden stands providing seating accommodation for 2,500. The pitch was surrounded by barriers and there were turnstiles and even a special entrance for carriages.

Pavilions and changing rooms were brought from Parkside and there was also a refreshment booth. The pitch was another area which was a vast improvement on Parkside. The playing surface was almost level and drained well.

In the hope of persuading more spectators to travel to the enhanced facilities at Lenton, Forest arranged for special omnibuses on matchdays and also for all trains passing through Lenton Station to stop there.

Over 2,000 watched the first game, a 4-1 victory over Stoke on Trent. It was a fine, dry day which no doubt boosted the crowd. In November, Forest played Notts County in a friendly, which County won 4-0 in front of a crowd of 10,000.

However despite more friendlies against glamour opposition being arranged, Forest still couldn't attract crowds of more than 2,000 that season.

FACT 8
1888
FOOTBALL
LEAGUE REJECTION

In 1888 the Football League was formed, but Nottingham Forest's application to become one of the founder members was rejected.

In March of that year officials of Burnley sounded out other clubs about forming a league so that regular fixtures against each other could be guaranteed. A total twelve clubs from the North and Midlands got together and agreed to meet the following month in Manchester to formalise the rules.

At the next meeting, Forest applied along with Sheffield Wednesday and Halliwell to join. Forest argued that they were of equal playing standard to most of the others involved. A lengthy debate followed and Forest had some support from others. However all three were rejected due to there not being enough dates in the calendar when the FA and county cup competitions were taken into account.

Forest were invited to join other clubs who were considering the formation of a second league but declined to do so. In 1888-89 they continued to play friendlies and took part in the FA Cup but were disappointingly beaten by Chatham in the second round.

FACT 9

1889
FOOTBALL
BY WELLS LIGHT

Nottingham Forest experimented with artificial lighting in a friendly with Notts Rangers at the Lenton Ground on 25th March 1889. The game kicked off at 7.45pm and was played under Wells lights.

Fourteen large blowlamps, often seen in shipyards and ironworks, were placed around the ground. Both teams were in bright colours and a white ball was used to aid vision.

Watched by 5,000 spectators, it was a keenly contested game which Notts Rangers, who were supposedly of a lower standard than Forest, won 2-0. Forest had plenty of possession but were not able to test the opposition keeper until late on in the game.

The lights were effective but if it got windy, the flames blew in other directions leading to dark shadows being cast. This made it difficult for the officials to spot any infringements unless they were very close to the play.

While the game itself had been entertaining and even some rain didn't reduce the spirits of the crowd, the cost of the fuel for the lights meant the experiment was not repeated again.

FACT 10
1889
PROFESSIONALISM &
THE FOOTBALL ALLIANCE

Nottingham Forest turned professional in 1889 and also joined the newly formed Football Alliance, an unofficial second tier of the Football League.

At the end of the 1888-89 season clubs at the bottom of the Football league had to apply for re-election and did so successfully. Nine who had hoped to take their places met in Manchester and agreed to form their own competition, the Football Alliance.

With three vacancies available, Forest applied by letter and were accepted. The new league effectively ended the short-lived Football Combination, which was badly managed and failed to have any proper fixture structure.

Forest's application had been helped by the fact a few weeks earlier, committee members had agreed to players being paid. Over the course of the previous season, they had struggled on occasions to raise a team due to amateurs having other commitments.

On 7th September Forest played their first game in the new competition, when they won 3-1 at Walsall Town Swifts. However, they struggled for most of the season and had some heavy defeats, including a 12-0 thrashing at Small Heath. They won just three out of 22 games and finished second from bottom.

FACT 11
1890
THE
TOWN GROUND

Nottingham Forest moved back to the Trent Bridge area in 1890, developing a ground at Woodward's Field.

Forest had been at Lenton for seven years. The first two of these were at Parkside before moving to the Gregory Ground in 1885. Spectators had always been reluctant to travel out there and with the club now having to pay wages, they decided to move back to a more populous area.

Woodward's Field stood where Bunbury and Woodward Streets are now. Forest spent £1,000 levelling the pitch, creating banking and a 1,000 seat stand on one side of the ground. This stand was unusual in that it was arc shaped, so spectators did not have to crane their necks to see what was happening in the corners.

Press reporters were impressed at the new ground which gave them covered accommodation and desks, unlike at Lenton where there were no such luxuries.

The first game at their new home, which Forest re-named the Town Ground, was against Queens Park on 3rd October 1890. The Mayor, Alderman Goldschmidt, kicked the game off in front of an enthusiastic crowd of 3,500. In an entertaining game Forest came from 2-1 down to win 4-2.

FACT 12
1891 RECORD VICTORY

Nottingham Forest recorded their best-ever victory on 17th January 1891 when they thrashed Clapton 14-0 in the first round of the FA Cup.

A special train ran to London carrying Forest supporters to this tie, which took place at the Spotted Dog Ground in Upton. Clapton were one of the strongest sides in London at the time, but they were without some key players for the game.

On a hard, frosty surface, Forest took the lead in the first minute through Arthur Shaw. They quickly added two more from Smith and Alex Higgins to build a comfortable early lead. Shortly before half time Neil McCallum scored two in quick succession to lead 5-0 at the break.

In the second half Forest completely destroyed the home side, scoring a further nine goals. Lindley and Smith completed hat-tricks while Higgins took his match tally to four. Shaw, who had opened the scoring, got the fourteenth and last of the game just before full time.

In the following round Forest needed two replays to beat Sunderland Albion, before losing 4-0 at Sunderland in the quarter final. As well as the 14-0 win being Forest's record victory, it is also an all-time record away win in the FA Cup.

FACT 13
1892
THE LAST FOOTBALL ALLIANCE CHAMPIONS

Forest won the Football Alliance in 1891-92, the last season of its existence prior to the expansion of the Football League.

Forest were unbeaten in their eleven home games. Their best result was a 7-0 thrashing of Burton Swifts. Only Grimsby Town scored more than one goal against Forest on their home turf, in a game that was drawn 3-3.

Away from home Forest lost three times, but crucially they avoided defeat at closest title challengers Small Heath and Newton Heath. They eventually won the title by two points. In honour of their success, the Sheriff of Nottingham hosted a special dinner where all guests wore red buttonholes.

That summer the Football League increased in size, absorbing the Football Alliance into it. Forest were rewarded for their title success and elected into an expanded sixteen team First Division.

Forest's first game in the Football League ended in a 2-2 draw at Everton. It was a historic day for the home club too, as it was the first league fixture at their new Goodison Park ground. Forest lost their next three games but improved as the season continued to finish in tenth place.

FACT 14
1898
THE EAST MIDLANDS FA CUP FINAL

Forest won the FA Cup for the first time in 1898. They beat Derby County 3-1 in the final at Crystal Palace in London but had to borrow their opponents' shirts afterwards for the photographs.

Forest reached the final with victories over Grimsby Town, Gainsborough Trinity, West Bromwich Albion and Southampton. For both clubs it was their first final with special trains run from all over the Midlands.

The crowd of 62,017 was less than the 80,000 expected. Arthur Capes gave Forest a twentieth minute lead but after half an hour Stephen Bloomer scored with a header to equalise. Three minutes before half time Capes restored Forest's lead.

The second half was not as entertaining as the first, but all that mattered for Forest was John McPherson adding a third with four minutes left. After the game, Forest's red shirts looked too dull for the photographs and they had to wear the white ones of Derby instead.

When Forest's players arrived back at Midland Station two days later, they were greeted by thousands of fans who lined the route to the Maypole Hotel where the celebration dinner took place.

FACT 15
1898
THE
CITY GROUND

Following the cup success, Nottingham Forest moved to a home befitting of the FA Cup holders in 1898 when the City Ground was opened.

Although the Town Ground had been a good home to them since 1890, it had its limitations as there was little space for expansion. In December 1897, the club committee started selling bonds to raise the £3,000 necessary to develop land on the other side of the River Trent in West Bridgford.

The new pitch was laid with high quality turf transported on barges from Radcliffe on Trent. The wooden main stand had a barrel roof and at the Trent end of the ground there was a narrow covered wooden shelter. On the east side, opposite the main stand, there was spectator accommodation that didn't quite run the full length of the pitch.

The first game was on 3rd September and attended by the Sheriff and high-ranking corporation officials. On a gloriously sunny day there was a crowd of 15,000 but they went home disappointed as Forest lost 1-0 to Blackburn Rovers.

Forest's new home was welcomed by the football authorities and between 1899 and 1905 four FA Cup semi-finals were staged there. It also hosted an England v Wales international in 1909. The City Ground is now all seated with a capacity of 30,445.

FACT 16

1903
RECORD VICTORY
OVER DERBY

Forest's biggest victory over Derby County was on 14th November 1903, when they won 6-2 in a First Division fixture at the Baseball Ground.

The *Nottingham Journal* described the match as an extraordinary one, reporting that Derby had more possession, but that Forest seemed to score with every attack. Forest's defence was said to be in "wonderful form" while Derby's was "feeble and vacillating."

Rain restricted the crowd to 5,000. Forest were 2-0 up within three minutes thanks to goals from Sidney Sugden and Billy Shearman. Derby pulled a goal back from a free kick but Grenville Morris scored Forest's third after 23 minutes and it remained 3-1 at half time.

Derby dominated the opening stages of the second half and Hail headed home from a free kick to reduce the deficit. However, within a minute Shearman restored Forest's two goal advantage from a corner. Alf Spouncer then made it 5-2 and also scored the sixth when his shot from forty yards was caught by the keeper who then dropped it into his own net.

Later in the season Forest hammered Derby again at the City Ground, winning 5-1. The 6-2 victory remains Forest's biggest in the fixture and the highest away win by either side.

FACT 17
1905 SOUTH AMERICA TOUR

Forest went intercontinental in the summer of 1905 when they undertook a tour of South America.

A party of thirteen players, accompanied by Secretary Harry Hallam and vice president H S Radford sailed from Southampton on a journey that took three weeks. They went as guests of the Argentine FA, who paid the club £200 to visit. Forest were only the second English club to visit South America, following on from Southampton the year before.

The first game on 11th June was in the Uruguayan capital of Montevideo, where Forest beat Penarol 6-1. After that they were in Rosario, Argentina, beating the local side Rosario Central 5-0.

Buenos Aires was the venue for the remaining six games of the tour. Forest had big wins in all of them; 7-0 versus Belgrano, 13-1 versus Britanicos, 6-0 versus Rosario Central, 6-0 versus Alumni, 5-0 versus Argentinos and 9-1 versus Liga Argentina.

Considering Forest had finished third from bottom of the First Division, Hallam may have been polite when he suggested to Argentine officials that their teams were of Second Division standard. However, he was not wrong when he predicted a bright future for football in the country.

FACT 18
1906
RELEGATED ON
GOAL AVERAGE

Nottingham Forest were relegated from the First Division in 1905-06 due to the finest of margins. They were level on points with Middlesbrough but had a slightly inferior goal average.

In 1904-05 Forest escaped relegation by the skin of their teeth, finishing just a point ahead of Bury. The Lancashire side, along with Forest's neighbours Notts County, were then unexpectedly reprieved when it was decided to expand the First Division to twenty clubs.

Despite this narrow escape, Forest failed to strengthen and were made to pay for it. Their defence was much weaker, conceding eighteen more goals and there was not enough squad depth to cover injuries.

Forest's form at the City Ground, where they won eleven times, always looked set to keep them up. It seemed most likely that either Bury or Middlesbrough would join Wolverhampton Wanderers, who were well adrift at the bottom, in the Second Division.

Even going into the last game of the season Forest's fate remained in their own hands. They were on 31 points, while Bury and Middlesbrough both had thirty. Forest were beaten 4-1 at Everton, Bury beat Sunderland 3-0 and Middlesbrough drew 1-1 at Blackburn. It meant Forest were relegated for the first time in their history, thanks to Middlesbrough having a goal average of 0.789 to their 0.734.

FACT 19
1907
NEW YEAR SURGE
TO PROMOTION

Promotion straight back to the top-flight was secured in 1906-07. After a shaky start, they were unbeaten in their last seventeen games and finished the season as Second Division Champions.

After failing to win any of their first three games, a 3-0 victory at home to Leeds City was the start of a four-match winning run. After the Christmas and Boxing Day fixtures they were second in the table, but only two points separated the top four sides.

Forest suffered unexpected defeats to Grimsby and Port Vale, then were knocked out of the FA Cup by Barnsley. However, they then remained unbeaten for the rest of the season, winning fifteen and drawing two of their last seventeen games.

The *Nottingham Evening Post* described their form in the second half of the season as "brilliant in the extreme." Promotion was secured on 13th April with a 3-1 home win over West Bromwich Albion, which ended their opponents' faint hopes of going up.

Forest didn't ease up, winning their last two games to secure the Championship. The players were presented with their medals at a special dinner at the George Hotel, attended by the Mayor and Sheriff.

FACT 20

1911
UNLUCKY THIRTEEN
SENDS FOREST DOWN

Nottingham Forest were relegated in 1910-11. A series of failings in the second half of the season, in which they failed to win any of their last thirteen games, saw them finish bottom of the First Division.

Forest were unbeaten in their first four games and although they didn't maintain this throughout the autumn, they did not look in danger. After beating Tottenham 4-1 on Boxing Day, they were eighth in the table.

Whilst Forest's forwards were delivering the goods, the defence remained a concern. There was little communication between the back line while the goalkeeping position was particularly suspect.

In February and March, there were some calamitous decisions in the transfer market. Rather than sign a reliable keeper, three more forwards were signed instead. One of these, Jack Smith from Sheffield United, was suspended by the club for "inattention to training." There was another huge blow when leading scorer Grenville Morris was injured while playing for Wales.

After beating Liverpool 2-0 on 21st January, Forest lost twelve and drew one of their last thirteen games. Relegation was confirmed on 8th April when they were beaten 1-0 at home to Sheffield Wednesday. Their fate had been sealed with two games still to play.

FACT 21
1913
FOURTEEN
STRAIGHT LOSSES

Forest endured a miserable spell in the summer of 1913, losing their last eight games of one season and the first six of the next.

The losing run started on Good Friday, 21st March, when Forest were beaten 2-1 at home by Bradford Park Avenue. The following day they lost 2-0 at Birmingham then faced Park Avenue away on Easter Monday, losing 3-1.

1-0 defeats to Huddersfield at home and Leeds City away followed, before Grimsby won 2-1 at the City Ground. On 19th April Forest lost 2-0 at Bury and the season came to a close with a 4-2 home defeat to Fulham. The dreadful end to the campaign meant they only avoided having to seek re-election to the Football League on goal average.

The 1913-14 season then started as the previous one had ended. Forest's first two fixtures were at home but both ended in 3-1 defeats, to Leicester Fosse and Wolves. They then lost 5-1 at Fosse and 1-0 at Hull. A 2-0 defeat at home to Barnsley followed, then a 1-0 loss at Bury.

Forest finally ended the sequence on 4th October when they drew 1-1 with Huddersfield at the City Ground. They finished the season bottom of the league but were successfully re-elected.

FACT 22
1913
RECORD SCORER LEAVES

Nottingham Forest's all-time record goal scorer is Grenville Morris, who left the club in 1913. In fifteen years at Forest, he scored 217 goals in all competitions.

Morris was a Welsh international who joined Forest from Swindon for £200 in 1898. It was a huge fee at the time, but Forest were the FA Cup holders and showed that they wanted to remain as Nottingham's premier team. He immediately began justifying the fee with two goals on his debut.

Over the next fifteen seasons, he was a regular in the Forest side and finished as top scorer in seven of them. The most prolific season for Morris was 1906-07 when he scored 22 goals in 37 appearances.

Morris played at inside left where his dribbling and shooting skills made him able to cut inside, leaving defenders behind and score past the keeper. Morris remained at Forest despite two relegations, but he said his biggest disappointment was failing to beat Bury in the 1900 FA Cup semi-final.

Morris retired in 1913, having been planning for the future by starting a coal haulage business.

FACT 23
1918
FOREST KEEPER KILLED IN ACTION

Nottingham Forest's goalkeeper Tommy Fiske was killed in action at the Western Front in May 1918. He only played five games for the club, having been called up soon after the First World War broke out in August 1914.

Fiske joined Forest from Blackpool at the end of the 1913-14 season. Before the new campaign even started, Britain declared war on Germany and as an army reservist, Fiske was called up for duty and sent to France.

Forest's players and club officials received several letters from Fiske wishing them well and updating them on the action he was involved in. In November 1914 he suffered an illness and was sent back to a barracks in Southampton to recuperate. A letter he wrote said "I was lucky not to have been hit, I tell you, fellows all around me have been killed or wounded."

When Fiske recovered he played five games for Forest over the Christmas and New Year period, including two against Derby, before returning to his regiment.

In May 1918 Fiske was a sergeant with the Border Regiment fighting a German offensive at the Third Battle of the Aisne. He went missing in action and was presumed dead. His body was never knowingly found and he is mentioned on the Soissons Memorial.

FACT 24

1921
SEVEN
STRAIGHT WINS

Forest's longest winning sequence is seven in succession. One of the occasions they managed this was early in the 1921-22 season when they won promotion to the First Division.

The first game of the season on 27th August was lost 4-1 at Crystal Palace. However, two days later Bobby Parker's goal six minutes from full time gave Forest a 3-2 home victory over Hull City.

Forest then got revenge over Palace, beating them 2-1 at the City Ground before winning 1-0 against Hull at Boothferry Park. A double header with Coventry followed, with Forest winning 1-0 both at Highfield Road and then the City Ground.

On 24th September Forest made the short trip to Derby, winning 2-1 at the Baseball Ground in a game they dominated. A week later at the City Ground, Forest had a comfortable 3-0 victory over Derby to record their seventh straight win.

The winning run finally came to an end on 8th October in another East Midlands derby. Against Leicester City at Filbert Street, Forest trailed 2-0 but fought back for a draw, Noah Burton scoring the equalising goal in the last minute.

FACT 25
1922
SECOND
DIVISION CHAMPIONS

Promotion was won in 1921-22, finishing the season as Champions of the Second Division.

A 2-0 victory at Port Vale on 26th November 1921 took Forest back to the top of the table and they remained there for the rest of the season. They remained remarkably consistent, losing just once at the City Ground where they conceded just nine goals.

On the road Forest suffered back to back defeats on just one occasion, in February and early March. Jack Spaven finished as leading scorer with eighteen goals. He was the only player to reach double figures as the scoring was spread around the team.

Promotion was secured on 22nd April with two games still to go when they beat Stoke City 3-1 at home. The only regret about securing a return to the First Division after eleven years being the crowd, which was limited to just 12,000 due to torrential rain.

The following Saturday Forest beat Leeds United 1-0 at the City Ground to secure the Championship. They finished the season on 56 points; four clear of Stoke who also went up in second place.

FACT 26
1925
DOOMED TO RELEGATION

Nottingham Forest were relegated in 1924-25, finishing bottom of the First Division in a season they never looked like staying up.

Four straight defeats at the start of the season set the tone for the rest of the campaign. They were second from bottom at New Year but despite only trailing Burnley on goal average, they had played two games more.

Forest failed to win for the first three months of 1925, finally achieving a victory on 4th April, when they beat Leeds United 4-0 at the City Ground. Their plight was by now hopeless, as they were six points adrift of safety with six games to go.

The win against Leeds would be Forest's last of the season. Their fate was sealed in the middle of April. On the 14th they drew 0-0 at Blackburn and the following day, wins for Arsenal and Leeds left Forest eight points adrift with three games remaining.

Forest lost their last three games without even scoring a goal. Ironically, the last goal they conceded that dreadful season, in a 2-0 defeat at Aston Villa, was scored by Billy Walker, who would be manager when they finally returned to the top-flight 32 years later.

FACT 27
1937 RECORD DEFEAT

Forest suffered their record defeat on 10th April 1937. They were thrashed 9-1 by Blackburn Rovers in a Second Division fixture at Ewood Park.

Forest got off to an unlucky start in the first minute when keeper Percy Ashton pushed a shot on the crossbar only for the ball to bounce back over the line. They conceded two more in the next nine minutes before Arthur Betts missed a great opportunity to get one back.

After Betts' miss, Forest's midfield and defence simply crumbled, leading to them being 7-1 down at half time. Forest couldn't even score their goal themselves, instead it was an overhit header back to the keeper by a Blackburn defender.

In the second half Blackburn eased up somewhat but added two more. Forest had simply been overwhelmed by Blackburn's quick movement, passing and crossing. The report in the *Nottingham Journal* said their positional play was terrible and the keeper could not be at fault for any of the goals. The correspondent felt it was impossible for them to ever play so badly again.

The defeat left Forest nervously looking over their shoulders. They were third bottom of the table with four games remaining but did have two games in hand on Bradford City and went on to escape the drop.

FACT 28
1939
WAR BREAKS OUT
AS PLAYERS TRAVEL

Forest's players were on their way to a league fixture at Swansea City when the Football League was suspended due to the outbreak of the Second World War.

When Germany invaded Poland on Friday 1st September 1939, war was inevitable. Fixtures went ahead the following day, with Forest beating Newport County 2-1 at the City Ground in their third game of the season.

On the morning of Sunday 3rd September, Forest's players set off by train for Swansea, where they were scheduled to play on the Monday. The British government had given Germany an ultimatum to withdraw troops by 11am that day, otherwise the two countries were at war.

The decoration of war led to an immediate suspension on the gatherings of crowds for entertainment purposes. The Football League immediately suspended the competition, with all fixtures eventually being declared null and void. The Government soon recognised that sport could boost morale and regional competitions were allowed with reduced crowds.

Forest's finances were severely hit and they relied mainly on young amateur players for the duration of the war. Two senior Forest players were killed in the fighting; Samuel Grenville Roberts at Dunkirk and Harry Race in North Africa.

FACT 29
1946
UP ON
THE ROOF

When Football League action resumed after the end of the Second World War, demand was so great that some spectators tried to watch the game from the roof.

Forest's first home game of the 1946-47 season was against Newcastle United on 5th September. An advert placed in the *Nottingham Journal* by the club secretary the day before said that all seats had been sold and that the gates would be opened two hours before kick-off for general admission.

A crowd of 32,691 saw Forest lose 2-0. An additional twelve had climbed onto the roof of the terracing on the east side of the ground in the hope of watching the game for free.

Despite such a large crowd, there were just two policemen at the game, stood behind each goal. One was content to watch the action and applaud the play, but the other was determined to eject all of the freeloaders. He climbed onto the roof and, not trusting his boots on the corrugated iron, crawled to them on his hands and knees before ejecting them one by one.

FACT 30

1947
GROUND
FLOODED

The City Ground was flooded in March 1947 after the River Trent burst its banks.

Between 21st January and 10th March that year Britain suffered one of the harshest winters on record. The thawing of snow and frost, coupled with widespread heavy rain, led to flooding in many parts of the country. On Tuesday 18th March the Trent overflowed, flooding 9,000 households in the city.

At the City Ground, the pitch was under three feet of water. Forest players kept fit by training at Ollerton Colliery's ground while the following Saturday's home game with Bradford Park Avenue was postponed.

A week later Forest were away, playing Manchester City at Maine Road where they lost 2-1. The City Ground still remained under flood water, with a reserve fixture being switched to the opponent's ground.

On 5th April Forest finally returned to league action at home. In the first league fixture at the City Ground since 18th January, they beat West Ham 4-3. Two days later Tottenham were the visitors and beat Forest 2-0.

Due to the number of postponements the season was extended by six weeks. Forest finally completed their fixtures on 14th June, beating Bradford Park Avenue 4-0.

FACT 31
1949
RELEGATED TO THE
THIRD DIVISION

Despite winning three of their last four games Forest were relegated from the Second Division in 1948-49 as it was too late to save them from the drop.

After losing 2-1 at Sheffield Wednesday on 19th March, their chances of escaping the drop looked slim. With nine matches to play they were four points behind Leicester who also had three games in hand. Forest beat Leicester 2-1 on 9th April to narrow the gap and give them some hope.

On 30th April Forest enjoyed their biggest win of the season, thumping West Ham 5-0 at Upton Park. However survival was out of their hands as Leicester still had three games to play compared to Forest's one.

Leicester played their games in hand on successive days the following midweek, winning one and losing one. This meant that on the last day of the season, 6th May, Forest needed to beat Bury and hope Leicester lost at Cardiff.

Forest did beat Bury 1-0 and at the final whistle many fans invaded the pitch thinking they had survived. However the news came though that Leicester had scored a late equaliser to send Forest down. In some ways they had been desperately unlucky. Of 21 games lost, seventeen of them had been by the odd goal.

FACT 32
1951
RECORD BREAKING
PROMOTION SEASON

When Forest returned to the Second Division in 1950-51 they won the Third Division South and scored 101 goals, their highest ever tally.

Forest got off to a magnificent start, winning eight of their first nine games. After their first defeat of the season at Torquay they bounced back in style, hammering Aldershot 7-0 at the City Ground. This was the start of another nine-game unbeaten run that included a 9-2 home thrashing of Gillingham.

Two days before Christmas Forest lost 2-0 at fellow promotion hopefuls Norwich, a result that meant they now only led the table on goal average. With only the champions being promoted, there was little room for error. A 3-2 defeat at Southend on 10th April meant they were only one point ahead with eight games remaining.

While Norwich faltered, Forest had a near perfect end to the season. They won seven and drew one of those eight games to finish six points clear at the top. In the final game of the season, they won 3-2 at Swindon to go past the 100 goal mark. One of the goalscorers was Wally Ardron who took his tally to 36, still the highest by a Forest player in a single season.

FACT 33
1957
EAST MIDLANDS
PROMOTION DOUBLE

In 1956-57 Forest were promoted back to the First Division after 32 years away. They finished second in the table to ensure they went up alongside another East Midlands side, Leicester City.

Forest had a great start to the season, losing just one of their first ten games. They were top of the table at the end of September, ahead of Leicester on goal average.

By the turn of the year, Leicester had begun to pull away at the top, leaving Forest battling with nine or ten others who could reasonably hope to go up alongside them. They then hit form at the right time, going unbeaten in eleven games. This included 7-1 wins in successive weeks, away at Port Vale then at home to Barnsley.

The unbeaten run came to an end on 30th March, when Leicester beat Forest 3-1 at the City Ground. The Foxes were now ten clear at the top with five games to go. Forest were in third, but just a point behind Blackburn with two games in hand.

Forest emphatically made sure of promotion in their penultimate game. Needing just a point against Sheffield United at Bramall Lane, they cruised to a 4-0 victory. The *Nottingham Post* praised Forest's "high degree of consistency and on the ground football which brought handsome dividends."

FACT 34
1957
THE
BUSBY BABES

On 12th October 1957 a then record City Ground crowd of 47,654 watched Nottingham Forest play Manchester United. They put in a fine performance in a 2-1 defeat to the 'Busby Babes' just four months before the Munich air disaster.

Forest were second in the table after eleven games and two points ahead of reigning champions United. Their side contained a number of exciting young players who had come through the youth system hence the nickname of 'Busby Babes.'

United shocked Forest with a goal after just three minutes, David Pegg crossing for Liam Whelan to score with a shot that gave keeper Charlie Thomson no chance. Forest dominated the rest of the first half and were denied a penalty after what looked a clear handball by Bill Foulkes.

Two minutes after the restart Forest got a deserved equaliser, Stewart Imlach heading in a cross from Johnny Quigley, but against the run of play Dennis Viollet scored again for United. Forest were deflated but they still had some chances to equalise that were off target.

Both teams were given a huge ovation at the end. The following February, six of the players who played for United on the day were amongst 23 who died when their plane crashed at Munich airport on the way back from a European tie in Belgrade.

FACT 35
1959
TEN MEN FOREST
WIN THE FA CUP

Forest won the FA Cup for the second time in 1959. They beat Luton Town 2-1 in the final at Wembley, despite having to play for an hour with ten men.

The two finalists were only separated by four places in the league table that season but for most of the first half at Wembley it looked far more than that. Forest dominated the play and raced into a 2-0 lead in the first quarter of an hour.

Reg Dwight scored the first goal, hitting an unstoppable shot from a cross by Stewart Imlach. The second came when Billy Gray crossed for Tommy Wilson, who scored with a well-placed header.

After 32 minutes Forest suffered a serious blow when Dwight was stretchered off after breaking his leg. With no substitutes allowed, they had to see out the rest of the game with ten men.

Luton pulled a goal back through David Pacey midway through the second half. With ten minutes remaining Forest were virtually reduced to nine men when Bill Whare developed cramp and stayed on the wing. Luton were dominant by this stage but Forest held on for victory.

Two days later, 150,000 fans lined the streets to watch a victory parade, where there was a special welcome for Dwight who appeared in a bath chair.

FACT 36
1961 FLOODLIGHTS INSTALLED

Floodlights were installed at the City Ground in 1961 but there was no glamour friendly to mark their switch on. Instead they were used for the first time in a League Cup tie with Gillingham.

During the 1950s many clubs installed floodlights but as they could not be used for Football League games, they arranged money spinning friendlies against top foreign opposition. By the time Forest opted to go ahead and paid £20,000 for their installation, they had been cleared for use in domestic competitions.

With a European game in Spain just two days away, changes were made to the team for this League Cup tie against Fourth Division opposition. Eighteen-year-old Charlie McGlinchey made his debut at outside left and reserve keeper Noel Wood was given a chance.

Geoff Bowden headed Forest into the lead after twenty minutes and Colin Booth made it 2-0 just before half time. Wood was largely a spectator in goal but he could do nothing about Bob Ridley's 54th minute effort that brought the Gills back into the game.

Forest continued to dominate but couldn't find a way past keeper John Simpson. Colin Addison finally did so with ten minutes remaining, heading in from a corner. Bowden scored a fourth with a minute left to take Forest into the next round.

FACT 37
1961 INTER CITIES FAIRS CUP

Nottingham Forest played in Europe for the first time in 1961-62, but their continental sojourn was a short one as they were eliminated in the opening round.

Despite only finishing fourteenth in the First Division in 1960-61, lack of interest from other clubs enabled Forest to be able to compete. They were given a tough draw in the preliminary round, being paired with Spanish side Valencia.

Forest flew out to Spain for the first leg on 12th September, the day after they had beaten Gillingham in a League Cup tie. There was little time for acclimatisation with temperatures touching ninety degrees and kick off only 24 hours away.

In front of 46,000 at the Estadio Mestalla, Brazilian international Waldo gave Valencia 2-0 half time lead. It could have been more but Forest keeper Peter Grummitt made a number of saves under pressure. In the second half Forest gave a better account of themselves but they couldn't reduce the deficit.

Forest remained confident of turning the tie around at the City Ground. However, their hopes of a comeback were dashed in the first fifteen minutes when Waldo scored twice. Forest trailed 3-0 at half time and eventually lost 5-1, going out 7-1 on aggregate to a team that went on to win the competition that season.

FACT 38
1967
SO CLOSE
TO GLORY

Arguably Nottingham Forest's greatest side apart from the Brian Clough era was that of 1966-67, which finished second in the First Division and reached the FA Cup semi-final.

Forest lost their first two games but Johnny Carey's exciting side found their form and steadily climbed the table. They won many admirers throughout the season with their free-flowing intense football and never say die attitude.

In March and April Forest won six successive games and were in second place, just a point behind Manchester United with five games remaining.

In the FA Cup, the moment to savour was in the sixth round when Forest were drawn at home to holders Everton. Forest won 3-2 with Ian Storey-Moore hitting a hat trick. However, the game was pivotal for other reasons, as Joe Baker suffered a first half injury that kept him out of the side in the coming crucial weeks.

Forest went on to lose the semi-final 2-1 to Tottenham Hotspur. In the league they won just two of those five remaining matches, eventually finishing four points adrift of United.

FACT 39

1967 RECORD GATE

The record attendance for a match at the City Ground was on 28th October 1967, when 49,946 saw Nottingham Forest beat Manchester United 3-1 in a First Division match.

Forest had finished as runners up to United in the title race the previous season. There was added interest to the game this time around because it was United forward Denis Law's last match for six weeks. He had been given a lengthy suspension for a bust up with Arsenal's Ian Ure at Old Trafford earlier in the month.

In a tremendous atmosphere, Joe Baker scored two headed goals in the first half to give Forest a 2-0 lead at the interval. He almost completed his hat-trick straight from the restart but keeper Alex Stepney blocked his low shot.

The *Football Post* reported that the crowd broke into pandemonium after an hour when Forest went 3-0 ahead. Moore's shot was deflected over his own keeper by Paddy Crerand and Wignall followed in to help the ball over the line.

With 21 minutes remaining George Best dinked his way past three Forest players before hitting an unstoppable shot past Peter Grummitt. It meant a nervous last twenty minutes for Forest as United took control but Best and Law were unable to take their chances.

FACT 40

1968
MAIN STAND
FIRE

It was a miracle nobody was killed or seriously injured when Nottingham Forest's home game with Leeds United on 24th August 1968 was abandoned due to a fire in the Main Stand.

The fire began in a boiler room shortly before half time. As the players went down the tunnel there was a large crackle, the lights went out and they were told to head for the car park instead. Some Forest players had to barge a door down to find an exit and others turned back towards the pitch.

Fans were led to safety in what *The People* described as "A magnificently controlled evacuation." Within minutes the whole stand was ablaze, showing just how close it had been to a major tragedy. Amazingly the only injuries were minor ones to a television crew who had to scramble down from the gantry.

The whole stand was gutted, including all the takings at the turnstiles and £40,000 of television camera equipment. Many of the club's records and memorabilia were also destroyed.

Forest had to play their next six games at Notts County's Meadow Lane ground, failing to win any of them. The rearranged game with Leeds was played the following February, the visitors winning 2-0.

FACT 41
1970
RECORD APPEARANCE
HOLDER LEAVES

Bob McKinlay, Nottingham Forest's record appearance holder, retired in 1970 after 692 appearances in all competitions.

McKinlay was the nephew of Billy McKinlay, who played over 350 games for Forest before the Second World War. He made his debut as a teenager in 1951-52 but had to remain content with reserve team football until he established himself in the side in 1954-55. Two seasons later he helped Forest to promotion.

During the 1960s McKinlay showed remarkable consistency, playing in every league game for eight seasons out of nine. In the one that he didn't manage to play all 42 games, he played in 41 of them.

Amazingly, despite playing as a central defender, McKinlay wasn't booked until he had played over 400 games for the club. Even then it wasn't for dirty play, but for kicking the ball into the crowd after committing an infringement.

As a defender, McKinlay was firm but fair and played within the rules. Off the field he was a gentleman, always stopping to sign autographs for children who gathered in the club car park.

McKinlay retired from playing at the end of 1969-70 when he was 37 years old. He had a brief spell on the club coaching staff before becoming an officer in a youth offending unit. He died in 2002.

FACT 42
1971
THE GOAL THAT WASN'T

On 28th August 1971 Forest earned a draw against Crystal Palace at Selhurst Park thanks to the honesty of the opposing captain. After a goal was awarded for a shot that had hit the side netting, Steve Kember backed up the claims of the furious Forest players.

The two sides were drawing 0-0 at half time but Palace took an early lead after the restart when Alan Birchenall scored from close range. Within four minutes Forest were level thanks to Duncan McKenzie, who seized upon a weak back pass to score.

With fifteen minutes remaining, Terry Wharton's low drive was deflected into the side netting by Bob Chapman. Forest's players were stunned when the linesman signalled for a goal and referee Ron Judson, who had been catching up on play, pointed to the centre circle.

Forest manager Matt Gillies joined his players on the field to protest and the game was held up for five minutes. After speaking with the linesman and inspecting the goal netting, Judson went to speak with Kember. The Palace captain gave an honest answer and a corner was then awarded instead.

The game finished 1-1 and Kember told reporters afterwards that he had to tell the truth, otherwise he would have understood if Forest refused to restart the game.

FACT 43
1972
RELEGATED

Nottingham Forest endured a miserable season in 1971-72 and were relegated after fifteen years in the First Division.

Despite just two wins in their first sixteen games, Forest remained just outside the relegation zone at the end of October. By New Year they were in the bottom two, but survival was not impossible.

A 1-0 home defeat to fellow strugglers Crystal Palace on 8th January was a huge blow. It was the start of a sequence of seven straight defeats. The last of these, 2-0 against Ipswich at the City Ground, was watched by 9,872 fans, the lowest league crowd for seventeen years.

Afterwards angry fans gathered outside calling for the committee to resign. Forest were adrift at the bottom seven points from safety and had just sold Ian Storey-Moore without having a replacement lined up.

Although Forest did have a mini revival it came too late. The inevitable relegation was confirmed in their penultimate game, when Wolves won 3-1 at the City Ground.

The committee stood by Matt Gillies as manager, but after calls for him to go intensified, he resigned in October and was replaced by Dave Mackay.

FACT 44
1973
NEW
CLUB CREST

In 1973 Nottingham Forest fans were invited to design a new club crest to replace the one they had been using since 1947.

Nottingham Forest began wearing a club crest on their shirts in the seasons after the Second World War, when a variation of the city's Coat of Arms was used. The only difference to the Coat of Arms was the abbreviation N.F.F.C. where the castle usually would be.

By the early 1970s, as commercialism in football slowly increased, Forest faced problems with copyright so needed a new design. In 1973 a competition was launched to design a new crest and the winner was David Lewis. A graphic design lecturer from Trent Polytechnic, he had already designed the Nottinghamshire County Council badge.

In Lewis's winning design a tree represents the Forest. Underneath that are wavy lines which are a tribute to the River Trent, then at the bottom is the word 'Forest'. It was first used on the club shirts in 1974 in addition to all club stationary, ties, flags and other souvenirs.

As well as having the honour of designing Forest's new crest, Lewis also won £25. The only addition to the crest since 1973 is two stars above the tree, indicating the two European Cup wins.

FACT 45
1974
ENGLAND'S FIRST
BLACK INTERNATIONAL

Viv Anderson, the first black footballer to play for England, made his Nottingham Forest debut on 21st September 1974.

Forest gave Anderson a chance after he was released by Manchester United and he impressed for the reserves during the 1973-74 season.

Aged eighteen, Anderson got an opportunity at right back against Sheffield Wednesday at Hillsborough when several players were struck down with illness. He impressed so much that Wednesday's left winger Eric Potts was switched to the other flank for the second half of a game Forest won 3-2.

It was after Brian Clough's arrival that Anderson really excelled. Clough taught him that the best way to respond to the racist chanting that was so common then was to ignore it and let his football do the talking. Anderson did just that and after starring in Forest's Championship winning side in 1978, he was selected to play for England against Czechoslovakia that November.

Anderson went on to make thirty appearances for England. It probably would have been many more had it not been for competition from Liverpool's Phil Neal in his position. He was named in the squads for two World Cups and one European Championships.

After 328 league appearances for Forest, Anderson left in 1984 when he joined Arsenal. He is widely regarded as Forest's best-ever right back.

FACT 46
1975 BRIAN CLOUGH

Brian Clough was appointed as manager of Nottingham Forest in January 1975. It was the start of an eighteen-year reign in which he would take them from the second tier to European Cup winners, and back again.

Clough had won the Championship with Derby in 1972. However this was followed by an uninspiring stint at Third Division Brighton and disastrous 44 days in charge of Leeds United. Clough took over from Alan Brown, who was sacked following a 2-0 home defeat to Notts County.

It was the arrival in 1976 of Clough's former assistant at Derby, Peter Taylor, that was a catalyst for success. Clough was the motivator, while Taylor the man who could spot potential. Together they moulded a team that included players who had been languishing in the reserves or had been surplus to requirements at bigger clubs.

Under Clough Forest won promotion in 1977, the Championship in 1978, then European Cups in 1979 and 1980. During Clough's time in charge there were also four League Cup wins but the FA Cup always eluded him.

After Taylor's departure in 1982 Forest never quite hit the heights and Forest slowly fell from grace. When Clough retired in 1993, he did so as manager of a side who were relegated.

FACT 47
1975
MCGOVERN & O'HARE RESCUED FROM LEEDS

In February 1975 Brian Clough made his first two major signings for Nottingham Forest, bringing two of his former Derby players out of the Leeds wilderness.

John McGovern, a defensive midfielder and John O'Hare, a forward, were both signed by Clough for Leeds from Derby. However both were frozen out after Clough's sacking and when they joined Forest, it was for just half the fee Leeds had paid for them.

McGovern was soon appointed as Forest's captain and helped the club to promotion from the Second Division in 1978 and the League Championship the following year. Injury prevented him lifting the League Cup in 1978 but he held aloft the European Cup in both 1979 and 1980.

One of McGovern's finest performances in a Forest shirt was the second leg of the 1979 European Cup semi-final in Cologne. He ran the game as Forest won 1-0 to progress to the final. McGovern was never capped by Scotland despite his success with Forest. After 337 appearances he left in 1982 to move into management with Bolton Wanderers.

O'Hare was 28 years old when he signed and used more sparingly, He did come off the bench in the 1980 European Cup final and retired from playing the following year. Both former players retain their links with Forest in ambassadorial and hospitality roles.

FACT 48
1976 ANGLO SCOTTISH CUP WINNERS

In 1976 Nottingham Forest won the Anglo Scottish Cup — a much-derided competition, but Brian Clough knew its importance for the future.

Forest finished top of their English a group, which also included Notts County. They then beat Scottish side Kilmarnock in the two-legged quarter final, winning 2-1 at home then drawing 2-2 away. In the semi-final they faced Scottish opposition again, winning the home leg against Ayr United 2-1 and the away game 2-0.

The final was an all English affair against fellow Second Division side Orient. The first leg took place on Monday 13th December at Brisbane Road. Forest dominated but couldn't add to John Robertson's first half penalty. Orient then snatched a draw with an injury time goal.

The return leg at the City Ground was just two days later. This time Forest made no mistake in front of goal and led 3-0 at half time thanks to two goals from Colin Barrett and one from Sammy Chapman. Forest continued to dominate in the second half with Ian Bowyer scoring to complete a 4-0 win.

Although many teams did not take this competition seriously, Clough thought differently. He felt it could provide a springboard for future successes and he would be proved right.

FACT 49
1977
PROMOTED WHILST ON A PLANE

Nottingham Forest's players were flying off on their holidays when their promotion to the First Division was confirmed at the end of the 1976-77 season.

Forest played some entertaining football but dropped points at times in games they were expected to win. They ended their season on 7th May having collected 52 points, but Bolton were four points behind and still had three games left to play.

Brian Clough refused to be despondent. He wrote in the *Football Post* "We have had a magnificent season by our standards. The future is bordering on exciting. I believe our genuine supporters recognise the fact that at some time in the future we will really take off."

On 14th May Forest's players departed from East Midlands airport for a ten-day break in Majorca. When they landed, they were informed that Bolton had been beaten 1-0 at home by Wolves. This meant there was no way Forest could be caught and that they would be playing in the First Division the following season.

Forest may have only just claimed the last promotion place but over the next three seasons Clough delivered success that no fan could ever have dared dream of.

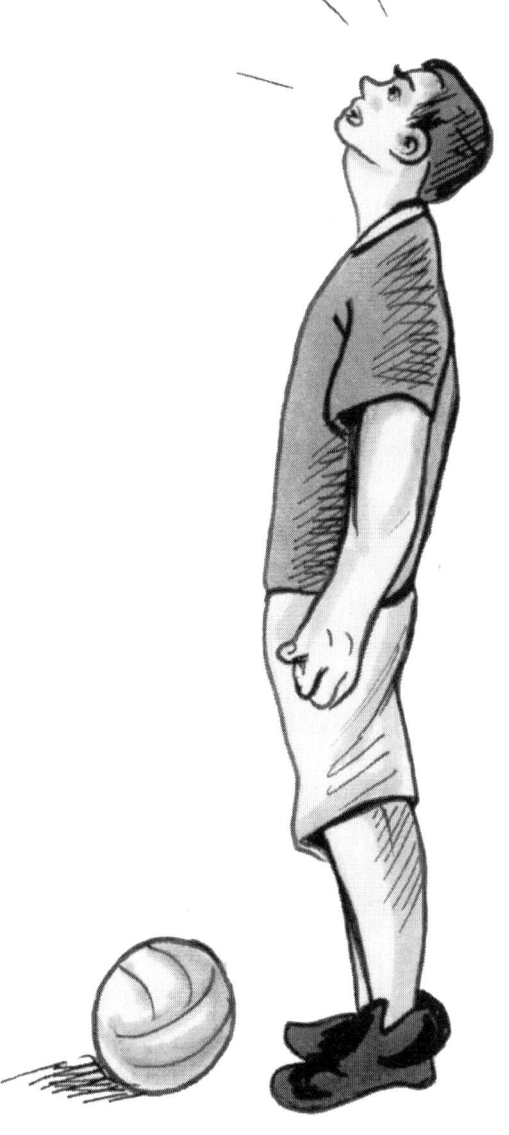

FACT 50
1978 LEAGUE CUP WINNERS

Forest's first major trophy of the Brian Clough era was won on 22nd March 1978, when they beat Liverpool 1-0 at Old Trafford in the replayed final of the League Cup.

The teams had first met at Wembley four days earlier in a game that ended 0-0. Forest's hero that day was eighteen-year-old keeper Chris Woods, who made a number of important saves as Liverpool dominated play early in the second half. Woods was in the side as regular keeper Peter Shilton was cup tied.

At Old Trafford Forest had much more of the play. Peter Withe missed a great chance in the fifth minute, heading wide from a cross by Tony Woodcock. Martin O'Neill also found himself clean through on goal but shot straight at Ray Clemence.

In the 53rd minute John O'Hare was brought down by Phil Thompson and a penalty was awarded. John Robertson converted the kick and there was no further scoring.

Afterwards a furious Thompson said he had deliberately brought O'Hare down knowing it was outside the area. Television replays showed that to be correct but in 210 minutes Liverpool had failed to score against a rookie keeper. Forest, who also had Archie Gemmill and David Needham cup tied and John McGovern injured, had fully deserved their victory and more success was to come.

FACT 51
1978 FOOTBALL LEAGUE CHAMPIONS

Nottingham Forest defied the odds in 1977-78, finishing as Champions of the Football League in their first season after securing promotion.

Forest were tipped to struggle with a squad that was a mixture of youngsters, journeymen and players who had failed to live up to their potential at bigger clubs. The only player to be signed in the close season was Kenny Burns, who arrived from Birmingham City for £150,000.

Forest won their first three matches and although they then lost 3-0 at Arsenal, they got back to winning ways the following week. A 4-0 victory over Ipswich at the beginning of October took them to the top of the table where they stayed for the remainder of the season.

Clough had further strengthened the squad in September with the signing of England international keeper Peter Shilton from Stoke and midfielder Archie Gemmill from Derby.

After a 1-0 defeat at Leeds on 13th November 1977 Forest didn't lose another game all season. A 0-0 draw at Coventry on 22nd April confirmed them as Champions with four games still remaining.

Forest eventually finished with 64 points, seven ahead of second place Liverpool. Burns, who Clough converted from forward to defender, was named Footballer of the Year. No team has won the Championship in the first season after promotion since.

FACT 52
1978
RECORD
CHARITY SHIELD WIN

Forest's one and only victory in the FA's traditional curtain raiser to the new season was in 1978. They beat Ipswich Town 5-0, a winning margin that has not been matched since in what is now known as the Community Shield.

Forest led 2-0 at half time thanks to goals from Martin O'Neill and Peter Withe. Things could have been different though had Peter Shilton not been on top form, making stunning saves from Tommy Parkin and Brian Talbot.

A minute into the second half Forest were awarded a free kick after a foul on Withe. It was taken by John Robertson and met by Larry Lloyd who made it 3-0. O'Neill converted Robertson's cross for the fourth but he was denied the chance of a hat-trick when he was substituted soon afterwards.

Robertson completed the scoring three minutes from time, seizing on defensive hesitancy to steal the ball and score from the edge of the area.

Forest have not played in a Charity/Community Shield match since. The 5-0 victory was the biggest since Manchester City beat West Bromwich Albion in 1968. No team since then has won it by five goals.

FACT 53

1978
42 GAMES
UNBEATEN

When Nottingham Forest lost 2-0 at Liverpool on 9th December 1978 it brought to an end an amazing 42 game unbeaten league run that had lasted over a year.

The run started with a 0-0 draw against West Bromwich Albion at the City Ground on 26th November 1977. It was the first of 26 games unbeaten between then and the end of the season which saw them crowned as Football League Champions.

Forest drew the first four games of 1978-79, finally tasting victory on 9th September with a 2-1 home win over Arsenal. On 25th November they won 1-0 at Bolton, their sixteenth game unbeaten since the start of the season, ensuring they had gone a full calendar year without defeat.

When Forest went to Anfield for the crunch game with Liverpool on 9th December, they were six points behind but with two games in hand. However, Forest failed to cope with the home side's fluent passing. They rarely got out of their own half as Liverpool cruised to a 2-0 victory.

Forest eventually finished that season in second place, eight points behind Liverpool. Their record remained intact until 2004 when Arsenal went 49 games without defeat. In 2020 they dropped to third in the unbeaten record table, as Liverpool went 44 games undefeated.

FACT 54
1979
ENGLAND'S FIRST MILLION POUND PLAYER

In February 1979 Trevor Francis was hailed as the first £1 million transfer in English football when he joined Nottingham Forest from Birmingham City.

Francis had made his Birmingham debut in 1971 as a sixteen-year-old but for three years had been seeking to move on due to their inability to compete for trophies. With Birmingham bottom of the league and relegation looking inevitable they granted Francis his wish, providing a club would meet their £1 million asking price.

With only Coventry being the only other club willing to match the price, Forest were able to seal the deal. Brian Clough often said he paid £999,999 to stop the fee going to Francis's head but the reality is with taxes and fees the total outlay was nearer £1.15 million.

Within a few months Francis had gone a long way to repaying his fee when he scored the only goal in the European Cup final. The following season he got crucial goals in the quarter and semi-final s as Forest retained the trophy although he missed the final through injury.

Francis's time at the City Ground was disrupted by injuries and arguably he failed to reach his full potential. However, the fee was recouped in September 1981 when he was sold to Manchester City for £1.2 million.

FACT 55
1979
RETAINING
THE LEAGUE CUP

Nottingham Forest won the League Cup for the second year running in 1979. They came from behind to beat Southampton at Wembley on 17th March, becoming the first team to retain the trophy.

Forest were the clear favourites to win the game but were nervous early on. They fell behind in the 16th minute when David Peach collected a through pass from Alan Ball and rounded Peter Shilton to score.

Six minutes into the second half Gary Birtles seized on defensive hesitation in the six-yard box to fire the ball into the roof of the net. On a heavy pitch Southampton wilted and with eleven minutes remaining Birtles won possession and burst through the defence to put Forest ahead.

Tony Woodcock put the game out of Southampton's reach with seven minutes to go, scoring from a tight angle from an Archie Gemmill cross. Nick Holmes gave Southampton a lifeline two minutes from time, scoring with a half volley from the edge of the area that gave Shilton no chance. However, their last desperate attack was thwarted by Larry Lloyd.

This was the 19th League Cup final and Forest had become the first team to retain the trophy. However, they failed to make it a hat-trick in 1980 when they lost the final 1-0 to Wolves.

FACT 56

1979 CHAMPIONS OF EUROPE

Just two years after being promoted from the Second Division, Nottingham Forest were crowned champions of Europe, beating Malmo 1-0 in the final in Munich.

Forest were given the toughest possible draw in the first round. They were paired with fellow English side Liverpool, who were in the competition as holders. Forest won the first leg 2-0 at the City Ground, Colin Barrett scoring a second late on as Liverpool chased an equaliser. They then defended resolutely to draw 0-0 at Anfield and progress.

Victories over AEK Athens and Grasshopper Zurich set up a semi-final tie with Cologne. A 3-3 draw at home in the first leg left Forest with an uphill task at the Mungersdorfer Stadium. However, Ian Bowyer's goal midway through the second half took Forest into the final.

Forest's opponents in Munich were Malmo of Sweden, who played defensively from the start. In first half injury time John Robertson crossed and Trevor Francis, who had been ineligible for the quarter and semi-final s, scored with a diving header to make it 1-0.

The second half wasn't spectacular, but it looked more likely Forest would add to their lead than Malmo score an equaliser. All that mattered though was that Forest's name was on the cup, a provincial English club had completed a meteoric rise to become Europe's best.

FACT 57
1980 EUROPEAN CHAMPIONS AGAIN

Nottingham Forest won the European Cup again in 1979-80, showing strength and determination to beat Hamburg 1-0 in the final in Madrid.

Forest made comfortable progress to the quarter finals, beating Osters IF and Arges Pitesti. They then lost the first leg of their quarter final 1-0 at home to Dynamo Berlin, only to come back and win 3-1 in East Germany. In the semi-final, three times champions Ajax were edged out 2-1 on aggregate.

Much of the build up to the final focused on Hamburg's English striker Kevin Keegan, twice European Footballer of the Year. Forest suffered a major blow in April when Trevor Francis suffered an Achilles tendon injury. His place for the final was taken by eighteen-year-old Gary Mills.

After twenty minutes John Robertson scored from the edge of the area after a one-two with Gary Birtles. Forest then defended deep, their five-man midfield frustrating Hamburg. Kevin Burns and Larry Lloyd were solid at the back and when the back line was breached, Peter Shilton didn't let the side down.

After the game Brian Clough had no time for anyone criticising his tactics, responding "We gave Hamburg a lesson in application, determination and pride. Defending well is just as important as attacking well. We weren't lucky, we were good."

FACT 58

1980
TWO EUROPEAN
SUPER CUP FINALS

Nottingham Forest's European Cup successes in 1979 and 1980 meant they contested the Super Cup against the winners of the Cup Winners Cup. Both two-legged ties were played during the calendar year of 1980.

The first leg of the 1979 Super Cup took place on 30th January 1980. Forest beat Barcelona 1-0 at the City Ground, Charlie George scoring the only goal in the ninth minute.

The return leg at the Nou Camp attracted a huge crowd of 80,000. Roberto Dinamite scored a 25th minute penalty but shortly before half time Kenny Burns made it 1-1. Early in the second half John Robertson had a penalty saved but Burns and Larry Lloyd were solid at the back as Forest held on for a 2-1 aggregate victory.

For the 1980 Super Cup, Forest faced Spanish opposition again. On 25th November, only 12,463 turned out at the City Ground to see Forest play Valencia. The visitors took the lead early in the second half but Forest hit back with two goals from Ian Bowyer.

At the Mastella Stadium on 17th December, Fernando Morena scored in the 51st minute for the home side. Despite the best efforts of Trevor Francis, returning after a long injury lay off, Forest couldn't find the net and Valencia took the trophy on away goals.

FACT 59
1980
THE
EXECUTIVE STAND

Nottingham Forest's new-found status saw a major improvement to the City Ground in August 1980 with the building of the Executive Stand.

The new structure replaced the old East Stand that had only been there for twenty years. However increased demand due to the playing success and improvements required under the Safety of Sports Ground Act made rebuilding necessary.

Designed by Sheffield architects Husband & Co, the stand had two tiers of seats divided by 36 executive boxes, which provided increased revenue from matchday hospitality. The seats were shiny red, except for the white ones that spelt out 'Forest' on the upper tier.

The stand could be seen from the city centre and was so big that it dominated the rest of the City Ground. It raised the seating capacity to 15,009 with a further 20,558 being accommodated on the terraces.

Brian Clough opened the stand prior to Forest's 2-1 win over Birmingham City on 20th August. After his retirement in 1993, it was renamed the Brian Clough Stand in his honour. Its current seating capacity is around 10,000.

FACT 60
1981 INTERCONTINENTAL CUP

On 11th February 1981 Nottingham Forest played in the first Intercontinental Cup final to take place as a one off in a neutral venue.

Traditionally a two-legged tie took place between the winners of the European Cup and Copa Libertadores to determine who was the club champions of the world. Forest declined to take part after winning the European Cup in 1979 as they were not keen on travel to South America, where crowds were often hostile.

When Toyota stepped forward with sponsorship and the solution of a one-off game in the Japanese capital city of Tokyo, Forest agreed to take part after winning the European Cup in 1980. Their opponents were Nacional of Uruguay, whose players were reported to have been offered a bonus of £5,000 per man to beat Forest.

On arrival in Tokyo, the players were shocked at the state of the pitch, which was badly parched. Jetlag was a problem too, with the game taking place at 12 noon local time, which was 3am to the players.

In front of a crowd of 62,000 that sat mostly in silence, Forest went behind after ten minutes but dominated the rest of the game. They were denied a penalty despite an obvious handball and the Uruguayans held out for a 1-0 victory.

FACT 61

1982
PETER TAYLOR
LEAVES

Brian Clough's assistant manager Peter Taylor left Nottingham Forest in 1982. An initially amicable parting turned sour a year later and the legendary pair never settled their differences prior to Taylor's death.

Taylor had been Clough's assistant at Hartlepool, Derby, and Brighton, then joined Clough at Forest in the summer of 1976. Clough was quoted as saying of his right-hand man "I'm not equipped to manage successfully without Peter Taylor. I am the shop window and he is the goods in the back."

In their six years at the City Ground, Clough and Taylor won promotion, the Championship, two European Cups and two League Cups. However, at the end of 1981-82 Taylor retired, wishing to spend more time in Spain.

Six months later Taylor was surprisingly appointed as manager of Derby. When Forest were drawn to pay at Derby in the FA Cup in January 1983, the two managers refused to shake hands. Relations broke down irreparably that summer when Taylor signed John Robertson from Forest.

In tabloid interviews Clough referred to Taylor as a "snake-in-the-grass." They never spoke again but when Taylor died suddenly in 1990 Clough was distraught and did attend his funeral. He also dedicated his autobiography to Taylor in 1994.

FACT 62
1982
PETER SHILTON MOVES TO SOUTHAMPTON

Another high -rofile departure from Nottingham Forest in the summer of 1982 was goalkeeper Peter Shilton, who had played a key part in recent successes.

Signed a month into the 1977-78 Championship winning season, Shilton was already an England international. He immediately added extra steel to Forest's defence and he conceded just eighteen goals from 37 appearances. He was voted PFA Player of the year by his fellow professionals at the end of the season.

Whilst at Forest Shilton also won two European Cups and one League Cup. His performances also helped him become England's first choice keeper ahead of Liverpool's Ray Clemence.

In 1981-82 Shilton was Forest's player of the season and he was also named in the PFA First Division team of the year for the fourth year in succession. He was preferred to Clemence for that summer's World Cup but with just one year left on his contract, speculation was rife about his future.

Brian Clough rated Shilton as the best goalkeeper in the World. The financial realities of the time though were that at 32 he was not getting any younger. When Southampton came in with a bid, it suited all parties for him to move to the South coast.

FACT 63
1983
JOHN ROBERTSON'S
DISPUTED TRANSFER

John Robertson, who made crucial contributions in both of Nottingham Forest's European Cup triumphs, left the club in 1983 in contentious circumstances.

Robertson made his debut for Forest as a seventeen-year-old in 1970. However, the midfielder had been transfer listed at the time Brian Clough came in as manager five years later. With the help of Peter Taylor, who gave him advice on diet, Clough converted him into a successful left winger who earned an international call up by Scotland.

Over a four-year period between 1976 and 1980 Robertson made 243 successive appearances. He scored the penalty that won Forest the League Cup in 1978 and the following year he provided the cross for Trevor Francis to score the only goal of the European Cup final.

In the 1980 European Cup final, Robertson scored the goal as Forest beat Hamburg 1-0. Clough would later write of Robertson in his autobiography "He became one of the finest deliverers of a football I have ever seen."

In 1983 Robertson was out of contract and opted to leave Forest for Derby. Clough, already livid that Taylor had gone back into management after saying he was retiring, was incensed at the £65,000 offered. The matter went to tribunal and Clough was vindicated when the fee was set at £135,000.

FACT 64
1984
CHEATED OUT OF
UEFA CUP FINAL

Nottingham Forest were beaten in the semi-final of the UEFA Cup in controversial circumstances in 1983-84. Years later, an investigation found that the referee had been bribed.

In the first leg against Belgians Anderlecht at the City Ground, two late headers from Steve Hodge gave Forest a 2-0 win against the side that had won the competition the previous season.

Two weeks later in Brussels, Forest were 1-0 down at half time to a brilliant long-range strike. After an hour, Anderlecht scored a penalty when the referee adjudged Kenny Swain had committed a foul. With two minutes remaining Anderlecht completed their comeback but in injury time Forest had a goal disallowed for pushing.

Thirteen years later, as part of a wider investigation into corruption in European football, it emerged that the Spanish referee had been paid 1.2 million Belgian francs. Anderelcht were banned from European competition for a year.

Those who played in the game recall how suspicious the two decisions were. Striker Gary Birtles told the BBC in 2016 "That penalty was the most embarrassing decision I have ever seen in football. The distance between Kenny Swain and their guy who went down was absolutely ridiculous." Paul Hart, scorer of the disallowed goal said "The whole thing stinks, it really does. When it's brought up, it still rankles."

FACT 65
1985 FATHER AND SON

Manager Brian Clough's teenage son Nigel became a Nottingham Forest regular in 1985-86. However, there was no question of favouritism as his performances over the next eight years showed he was more than worth his place in the side.

Nigel was eighteen when he was handed his first professional contract towards the end of 1984. Although he did make some appearances that season, it was an injury to Garry Birtles early in 1985-86 that gave him an opportunity for an extended run in the side. He didn't disappoint and finished the season as top scorer with eighteen goals.

In eight full seasons at Forest, Nigel finished as top scorer in six of them. He was rated so highly that Serie A side Pisa made a £1.5 million bid for him in 1988, but this was turned down. Comfortable in both midfield and attack, he was even used as an emergency defender during the 1992-93 season in which Forest were relegated.

In the summer of 1993 Nigel was sold to Liverpool. He had scored 131 goals for Forest, making him the second leading scorer in Forest's history. He returned on loan in 1996-97, scoring once in thirteen appearances as Forest were relegated from the Premier League again. He has since gone into management with Burton, Derby and Sheffield United.

1988
LEAGUE CENTENARY
TOURNAMENT

FACT 66

Forest were winners of a sixteen-team tournament held at Wembley in 1888 to celebrate the centenary of the Football League.

The tournament took place over a weekend in April. It involved eight teams from the First Division, four from the Second, and two each from the Third and Fourth Divisions. Qualification was based on league form earlier in the year.

All matches in the first two stages were forty minutes in length and Forest started off with an emphatic 3-0 win over Leeds United. Later that day they drew their quarter final 0-0 with Aston Villa before progressing on penalties.

The following day's games were sixty minutes in length. With only four teams left, the attendance dwindled to 17,000 from 41,000 on the first day. Forest played surprise packet Tranmere Rovers in the semi-final. An entertaining contest saw Forest twice come from behind to draw 2-2. They then progressed to the final on penalties.

The final against Sheffield Wednesday again went to penalties after a 0-0 draw. Forest won their third shoot-out of the tournament but there were hardly any fans left in the stadium as Stuart Pearce collected the trophy to bring a loss-making event to a close.

FACT 67

1989 LEAGUE CUP WINNERS

When Nottingham Forest won the League Cup for the third time in 1988-89. They came from behind to beat Luton Town 3-1 in the final and claim their first major trophy for nine years.

Forest beat Chester, Coventry, Leicester and QPR to set up a semi-final with Third Division Bristol City. The underdogs put up a brave fight, drawing 1-1 at the City Ground. The second leg finished 0-0 before Garry Parkers strike six minutes from the end of extra time took Forest to Wembley.

Relegation threatened Luton made it difficult for Forest and Mick Harford headed them into the lead in the 36th minute. Early in the second half the Hatters almost went 2-0 up but Brian Laws cleared Harford's effort off the line. Then Forest were awarded a penalty in the 54th minute when Steve Hodge was brought down by keeper Les Sealey. Nigel Clough stepped up to convert the kick and from then on Forest took control of the game.

In the 68th minute Clough dispossessed Luton's Kingsley Black, passed to Tommy Gaynor who then put Neil Webb through on goal. The Forest midfielder made no mistake, slipping the ball past Sealey. With fourteen minutes to go, Gaynor set up Clough for the third to seal a first trophy for nine years.

FACT 68
1989 HILLSBOROUGH

On 15th April 1989 Nottingham Forest met Liverpool at Hillsborough in Sheffield for the second year running in an FA Cup semi-final. The day ended in tragedy when 96 Liverpool fans were crushed to death at the Leppings Lane end of the ground.

The game was abandoned after six minutes when fans began to spill over the barriers onto the pitch. It was soon clear something was seriously wrong when advertising hoardings were being ripped down to use as makeshift stretchers.

Forest fans at the Kop end could only watch on helplessly as the tragedy unfolded with very little information forthcoming over the loudspeaker. The death toll mounted and the final total was 95, with another fan remaining in a coma for four years before his life support was switched off.

Just three weeks later the match was replayed at Old Trafford. Liverpool won 3-1, with Brian Clough admitting Forest were in a "no win situation" with most neutrals wishing to see Liverpool progress to the final.

The disaster continues to be marked in Nottingham. The thirtieth anniversary in 2019 was commemorated by a gathering in Old Market Square where there was a minute's silence followed by Liverpool's anthem 'You'll Never Walk Alone' being played.

FACT 69
1989
FULL MEMBERS
CUP WINNERS

Three weeks after winning the League Cup, Nottingham Forest were back at Wembley where they beat Everton 4-3 in the final of the Full Members Cup.

The competition, for teams in the top two divisions only, was started in 1985 to provide an extra trophy to play for due to English teams being banned from Europe following the Heysel Stadium disaster. This was only the second time Forest had taken part, having declined to enter in the first two seasons.

Forest entered at the last sixteen stage and had away wins over Chelsea and Ipswich to reach the semi-final. Second division Crystal Palace gave them a tough contest at the City Ground and the score was 1-1 with five minutes to go. Palace then had a player sent off and capitulated, goals from Neil Webb and Stuart Pearce securing Forest's place in the final.

Wembley was less than half full on 30th April, with just 46,606 fans being in attendance. Those present witnessed a thrilling game in which Gary Parker twice equalised for Forest to take the game into extra time. Lee Chapman gave Forest the lead for the first time in the game but Tony Cottee made it 3-3. With just three minutes remaining Chapman scored again to give Forest victory.

FACT 70
1990
A RECORD EQUALING
FOURTH LEAGUE CUP

Nottingham Forest retained the League Cup in 1989-90. They beat Second Division Oldham Athletic 1-0 in the final to join Liverpool as the competition's most successful team with four wins.

In the second round Forest needed away goals to beat Third Division Huddersfield. They then beat Crystal Palace, Everton and Tottenham on their way to a semi-final with Coventry City. After a 2-1 win at the City Ground, Forest drew 0-0 at Highfield Road to reach the final for the second season running.

Forest had lost seven out of their last ten games and came under some pressure in the first half. Steve Sutton saved well from Andy Ritchie while at the other end Franz Carr had a header turned around the post.

Four minutes into the second half Nigel Jemson was in the clear and although his first shot was saved by Andy Rhodes, the rebound fell back to him and he stroked the ball into the net. Oldham, playing their 61st game of the season after also reaching the semi-final of the FA Cup, were jaded and Forest held on comfortably for victory.

The victory was Forest's fourth in the competition and at the time they were its most successful club along with Liverpool. However, they have not won it since and Liverpool's total is now eight.

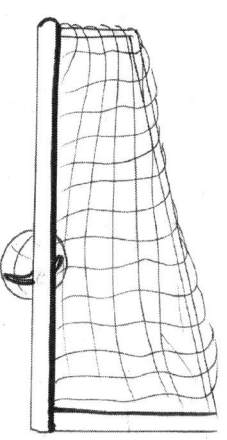

FACT 71
1990 NOTTINGHAM FOREST LADIES

In 1990 Nottingham Forest developed a ladies team, well before many other top flight clubs did.

The team was set up by ladies from Forest's community arm and they advertised in match programmes for more players. Further teams were also developed at junior levels. Their first taste of success came in 2000 when they won the East Midlands League Cup.

In the first decade after the Millennium, they enjoyed steadily increasing success, winning the East Midlands League, Midland Combination and FA Northern Premier League. They also began a virtual monopoly of the Nottinghamshire County Cup, having now won it thirteen times since 2004.

In recent years the team has been rebranded Nottingham Forest Women and developed a partnership with Trent University. A full-time general manager was also recruited to help further integrate the women's team into the wider club. Home games are played on a 3G pitch at Eastwood.

Nottingham Forest Women appointed a full time first team coach in 2019 as part of their efforts to move higher up the women's league system. Their current league, the FA Womens National League North, is the third tier. Home games are played on a 3G pitch at Eastwood.

1991
FA CUP
FINALISTS

The FA Cup was the one trophy that eluded Brian Clough. Despite bringing incredible success to Nottingham Forest they only reached the final once under his leadership and were beaten 2-1 by Tottenham Hotspur.

Forest took the lead in the sixteenth minute. Stuart Pearce scored from a free kick that was awarded after Gary Charles was scythed down by Paul Gascoigne. Shortly afterwards the Spurs midfielder was carried off on a stretcher, having ruptured his cruciate ligaments.

Nine minutes later Forest had a let off when Gary Lineker's goal was ruled out for offside, although television replays later showed the linesman was wrong to raise his flag. Gary Crosby then had a great chance to extend the lead but his effort was saved by Erik Thorstvedt. In the 33rd minute Mark Crossley brought Lineker down in the area then saved the subsequent penalty and Forest remained ahead at half time.

Spurs equalised through Paul Stewart in the 56th minute and had the better of the second half. Crossley made a magnificent one handed save from a David Howells header in the last minute, meaning the game went into extra time.

In the 94th minute Spurs went ahead when Stewart's header was helped into his own net by Des Walker. Forest couldn't find a way back and they have not reached the final since.

FACT 73
1992
WINNERS OF THE
LAST FULL MEMBERS CUP

Nottingham Forest were back at Wembley in 1992, when they won the Full Members Cup in the last year that the competition took place.

Forest were drawn away in every round of the northern section, beating Leeds, Aston Villa and Tranmere. They then faced Leicester City in the regional final, winning 2-0 at the City Ground after the first leg was drawn 1-1.

In the final against Southampton, Forest midfielder Scott Gemmill opened the scoring in the fifteenth minute. They then suffered a blow when captain Stuart Pearce was injured and had to be replaced by Steve Chettle.

Kingsley Black doubled the lead on the stroke of half time. However, in the second half Southampton hit back with goals from Matt Le Tissier and Kevin Moore to take the game into extra time. With five minutes remaining and penalties looming, Gemmill volleyed home from six yards to win the game for Forest.

Des Walker, who took over as captain when Pearce was injured, collected the trophy. With the creation of the Premier League, the Full Members Cup was scrapped after that season. Forest and Chelsea were the competition's two most successful sides with two wins each.

FACT 74
1992
THE FIRST TELEVISED PREMIER LEAGUE GAME

It was the dawn of a new era for English football in 1992-93 with the creation of the Premier League. The first of many live television games took place at the City Ground on 16th August 1992.

The Premier League allowed television revenues to be split amongst top-flight clubs rather than across all four divisions. A huge television deal was agreed with BSkyB, with sixty games a season to be screened exclusively on Sky Sports. This was treble the number that had been shown by ITV in 1991-92.

The first game to be shown live was Forest's opening game at home to Liverpool. Forest dominated the first half with Roy Keane and Nigel Clough in outstanding form. Had it not been for Liverpool keeper David James, Forest may have led by more than 1-0 at half time. James could do nothing about Teddy Sheringham's 28th minute goal, an unstoppable shot from the left of the area.

The second half was scrappier than the first, but Forest reasserted their authority late on. Brian Clough said of Sheringham's match winning goal "We don't work on scoring goals like that, they come out of the blue from pure ability. Edward Sheringham stuck it in... bang! That's what strikers are paid for."

1993
FACT 75 TEARS AS CLOUGH LEAVES & FOREST RELEGATED

After eighteen years in charge of Nottingham Forest, Brian Clough retired at the end of 1992-93, a campaign that saw them relegated from the Premier League.

The optimism generated by a 1-0 win over Liverpool in the first game of the season was soon lost. Teddy Sheringham, who scored the winning goal that day, was sold to Tottenham a week later. The failure to adequately replace him and defender Des Walker, who left for European Cup finalists Sampdoria in the summer, cost Forest dearly.

Forest lost their next six games after the opening day victory and by the turn of the year had won just three games. Midfielder Roy Keane was performing admirably, defender Stuart Pearce remained uncompromising and Nigel Clough tried his best up front, but too many players around them weren't good enough.

In February there was a brief revival and Forest climbed out of the relegation zone on goal difference. However, two wins from the next ten left them on the brink of going down.

In April Clough confirmed he would be retiring at the end of the season. On 1st May, Forest lost 2-0 to Sheffield United at the City Ground, which confirmed their relegation. There wasn't a dry eye in the stadium at the end as Clough waved goodbye for the last time.

FACT 76
1993 ANGLO ITALIAN CUP

The only time Nottingham Forest competed in the short lived Anglo Italian Cup they didn't even make it out of the East Midlands.

The competition ran for four years in the 1970s and was on an invitational basis, with Forest never entering. In 1992 it was reprised due to the scrapping of the Full Members Cup, with teams from the second tiers of England and Italy taking part.

To progress to the stage of playing against Italian clubs, Forest first needed to top a regional group of three teams. They were paired with local rivals Derby County and Notts County, playing each just once.

Fans were underwhelmed by the competition. The games were played in successive weeks in September, with Forest losing their opener 3-2 at Derby, who had earlier lost to Notts County by the same score line.

Forest could be sure of progress if they beat Notts County at the City Ground by two goals on 15th September. The game attracted a crowd of just 7,347, who saw Gary Lund give County the lead in the first half. Stan Collymore equalised after 54 minutes but the score remained 1-1 and Forest finished bottom of the group.

By the time Forest were back in the second tier in 1997, the competition had been scrapped.

FACT 77
1994
STRAIGHT BACK UP

Under new manager Frank Clark, Nottingham Forest won promotion straight back to the Premier League in 1993-94, finishing nine points ahead of their closest rivals.

In choosing Bran Clough's replacement, Forest turned to Clark who was a member of the 1979 European Cup winning team and had been manager at Leyton Orient.

Clark kept most of the players who had suffered relegation but brought in defender Colin Cooper from Millwall, winger David Phillips from Norwich and striker Stan Collymore from Southend.

Forest had a slow start and at the end of September were only two points above the relegation zone. However, they steadily improved and by New Year were just a point outside the play-off positions.

In February Forest picked up just one point from three games, which included a derby defeat at Notts County. In the first weekend of March though they beat Peterborough 2-0 at the City Ground. This was the first of five straight wins that lifted Forest into second place.

Promotion was secured on 30th April when Forest came from 2-0 down to win 3-2 at Peterborough. They had secured a return to the Premier League with two games to spare. Collymore was one of the key players of the season, finishing as top scorer in all competitions with 25 goals.

FACT 78

1995
BACK INTO EUROPE

Forest finished third on their return to the Premier League, meaning they would be playing in Europe for the first time since 1984.

Forest had a great start to the season and were second after eleven games. A poor run of form in autumn saw them fail to win in six games, and they also struggled after Christmas. Although the title challenge faded, they were never out of the top five all season.

Collymore was again the club's top scorer. He netted 22 times in the league, three more than he had managed in the promotion campaign. Highlights of the season included a 2-1 win over Manchester United at Old Trafford and 7-1 thrashing of Sheffield Wednesday at Hillsborough.

Forest were unbeaten in their last thirteen games and finished in third place, twelve points behind champions Blackburn Rovers. Their away form was impressive, the ten wins being the same number achieved by the 1977-78 Championship winning side.

It meant Forest would be competing in the UEFA Cup the following season, having been unable to compete after winning the League Cup in 1989 and 1990 due to the ban on English sides after the Heysel Stadium disaster.

FACT 79

1995
COLLYMORE LEAVES
FOR RECORD FEE

Stan Collymore left Nottingham Forest in the summer of 1995, joining Liverpool for a British record transfer fee of £8.5 million.

Eyebrows were raised at the £2.25 million fee when Collymore joined Forest from Southend United after less than a season there. Although he had a prolific strike rate, it was still ten times what Southend had paid for him.

Collymore was not fazed by moving from a team battling relegation to a promotion chasing one and his goals helped take Forest back to the Premier League. He was again not daunted by the increase in standards and helped Forest to European qualification.

Throughout the 1994-95 season speculation mounted over Collymore's future. Manchester United manager Alex Ferguson was an admirer but in January he signed Andy Cole from Newcastle instead for £7 million.

At the end of the season Collymore was offered a lucrative new contract but turned it down. Frank Clark said that he could be sold to anyone willing to pay £8.5 million, more than any British club had paid for a player. Liverpool met the asking price and Collymore joined them on 3rd July.

FACT 80
1996 UEFA CUP QUARTER FINALISTS

Nottingham Forest reached the quarter finals of the UEFA Cup in 1995-96 before losing out to the eventual competition winners.

In the first round, Forest were paired with Malmo, their opponents in the 1979 European Cup final. After losing the first leg 2-1 in Sweden, Bryan Roy's 69th minute strike at the City Ground was enough to take Forest through on away goals. Forest then played French opposition in both the second and third rounds, beating both Auxerre and Lyon 1-0 on aggregate.

In the quarter final Forest were drawn against Bayern Munich. The first leg also brought memories of the 1979 final, as it was played in the Olympiastadion. Jürgen Klinsmann scored after sixteen minutes but this was soon cancelled out by Steve Chettle. Mehmet Scholl restored Bayern's advantage before half-time but it finished 2-1, giving Forest some optimism for the second leg.

Back at the City Ground, Forest received what Frank Clark described as "an object lesson in counter attacking." Bayern led 2-0 at half time and ended up 5-1 winners, Steve Stone's goal five minutes from time being little consolation. Bayern went on to beat Barcelona and Bordeaux to win the trophy. Forest have not played in Europe since.

FACT 81
1997
TOO MANY DRAWS MEANS RELEGATION

The optimism of the last two seasons evaporated in 1996-97. Nottingham Forest were relegated from the Premier League, with sixteen drawn games being a major factor in their downfall.

A 3-0 opening day victory at Coventry was soon forgotten as Forest then failed to win any of their next sixteen games. The sequence finally came to an end the week before Christmas when Arsenal were beaten 2-1 at the City Ground, but Forest then lost 4-0 at home to Manchester United.

By now Frank Clark had been sacked and Stuart Pearce was caretaker player-manager. At the beginning of March Dave Bassett took charge, with Forest one place above the relegation zone.

Forest endured a miserable end to the season, failing to win any of their last eleven matches. Seven of these were drawn, including against fellow strugglers Sunderland and Middlesbrough. Southampton also won a six pointer 3-1 at the City Ground.

Forest finished the season bottom of the table, seven points adrift of safety. However, the Board retained faith in Bassett as manager and managed to hold on to key players in an attempt to make an immediate return to the top-flight.

FACT 82
1998
CAMPBELL & VAN HOOIJDONK GET FOREST BACK UP

Nottingham Forest won promotion straight back to the Premier League in 1997-98. The lethal strike partnership of Kevin Campbell and Pierre van Hooijdonk played a crucial role in helping Forest win the First Division Championship.

Dutch international striker van Hooijdonk had arrived from Celtic in a £4.5 million deal in March 1997 but was unable to help Forest avoid relegation. However, he immediately pledged to remain at the City Ground to help Forest regain their Premier League status.

Forest won their first four games of the campaign, including a 4-0 home win over QPR in which van Hooijdonk scored a hat-trick. The Dutchman brought out the best in Kevin Campbell, who had struggled in the relegation campaign. Over the season Campbell scored 23 times, with van Hooijdonk finishing as top scorer with 29.

The scorer of the goal that all but sealed promotion was Chris Bart Williams, who deputised for the injured Campbell against Reading on 26th April. He scored the winner against Reading with three minutes remaining to leave Forest six points clear of Sunderland with a better goal difference.

Two days later Sunderland lost, confirming Forest's promotion. On the last day of the season the title was secured with a 1-1 draw at West Bromwich Albion.

FACT 83
1999
VAN HOOIJDONK STRIKES AS FOREST GO DOWN

1998-99 was a forgettable season for Nottingham Forest. They were relegated from the Premier League for the third time that decade after Pierre van Hooijdonk refused to play at the start of the season.

When Kevin Campbell was sold in the summer of 1998, van Hooijdonk questioned the club's ambition and insisted that he had a contract clause allowing him to leave if he desired. The Dutch international failed to attend pre-season training and remained in Holland instead, attending sessions with NAC Breda to keep fit.

Forest won two of their opening three games, but then failed to win any of the next nineteen, leaving them rooted to the bottom of the table. Van Hooijdonk returned in October but failed to arrest the slide and when he did score an equalising goal at Derby, his teammates refused to celebrate with him.

Dave Bassett was sacked in January and replaced by Ron Atkinson. He started off by not even realising which was the Forest dugout in his first home game in charge against Arsenal. In his next City Ground game, Forest suffered a humiliating 8-1 defeat to Manchester United.

On 24th April Forest's relegation was confirmed when they lost 2-0 at Aston Villa. Despite winning their last three games, Forest still finished eleven points adrift of safety.

FACT 84
2000
A GOAL AFTER FOURTEEN SECONDS

The fastest recorded goal in Nottingham Forest's history was on 16th March 2000 when Jack Lester scored against Norwich after just fourteen seconds.

Lester had signed from Grimsby two months earlier, having impressed for them in a 4-3 victory over Forest. His goal against the Canaries at the City Ground was his first in a Forest shirt and was scored before many fans had even taken their seats.

Despite taking such an early lead, the game ended up finishing 1-1. Lester's only other goal in fifteen appearances that season was also in a 1-1 draw, away to Fulham.

Lester's appearances under David Platt, who signed him, were limited but when Paul Hart took over as manager in 2001 he adapted well into an attacking midfielder. In two seasons he scored fifteen goals from seventy games but was released in 2003 with the club in financial trouble.

After less than two seasons with Sheffield United Lester re-joined Forest, with Joe Kinnear paying £50,000 for him. He was back at the City Ground for three years which were disrupted by a knee ligament injury. He left in 2007 and signed for Chesterfield.

FACT 85

2001
THE
YOUNGEST PLAYER

In 2001 Craig Westcarr became Nottingham Forest's youngest ever player. However, his City Ground career never lived up to expectations.

Westcarr signed professional forms when he was fourteen. He played for the under 19's when they were managed by Paul Hart, who replaced David Platt as first team manager in the summer of 2001.

Hart gave Westcarr his opportunity on 13th October in a game against Burnley at the City Ground. Forest were leading 1-0 when Westcarr replaced David Johnson in the 83rd minute. He was sixteen years and 258 days old. He had a one on one chance against the keeper but failed to score.

Despite his early promise, Westcarr never made the grade at Forest. He made a further twenty substitute appearances and started just two games, scoring one goal. After loan spells at Lincoln City and Milton Keynes Dons, he was released in 2005 and has had a nomadic career since, never playing above League One level.

In 2013 Westcarr gave an interview to the *Nottingham Post* and had fond memories of his opportunity, saying "I was buzzing, it's probably one of the best feelings I've ever had. I'm still the youngest, still got that record and it's good to have, to be a part of history at such a massive club."

FACT 86
2005
DOWN TO THE THIRD TIER

In 2004-05 Nottingham Forest were relegated to League One. In doing so they became the first club to have been champions of Europe but drop to the third tier of their domestic league.

Manager Joe Kinnear was aiming for promotion but Forest failed to win any of their first nine games. The pressure grew and Kinnear resigned following a 3-0 defeat at Derby County on 11th December 2004 that left Forest struggling in the relegation zone.

Mick Harford stood in as caretaker manager until Gary Megson was appointed on 10th January. Megson had taken West Bromwich Albion from the brink of relegation to the Premiership, but he got off to a disappointing start. Forest lost his first game in charge 2-1 at home to Millwall, leaving them seven points from safety.

A run of three wins from four games, including the first away victories of the season gave Forest some hope. Then a crushing 6-0 defeat at Ipswich started a run of eight winless games that made the drop an inevitability.

Relegation was confirmed in the penultimate game of the season, a 2-1 defeat at Queens Park Rangers. The following week at the City Ground, Forest ended the season with a 2-2 draw at home to Gillingham, a result that meant the Gills would be joining them in League One.

FACT 87

2006
SIX STRAIGHT WINS
BUT NO PLAY-OFFS

Nottingham Forest won six successive league games towards the end of 2005-06. This was something that had never even been achieved in the Brian Clough era, but they still missed out on the promotion play-offs.

Forest had a difficult start to their League One campaign, finding themselves in the relegation zone after losing five of their first seven games. They slowly turned things around and were eighth by Christmas.

In January and February, Forest went seven games without a win. The last of these was a 3-0 defeat at Oldham that led to the dismissal of manager Gary Megson.

Reserve team boss Ian McParland and former Walsall assistant manager Frank Barlow took over on a caretaker basis for the rest of the season. Results improved immediately with a 2-0 win at Port Vale and 7-1 thrashing of Swindon at the City Ground.

Forest won six games in a row in March and April, lifting them into the play-off positions for the first time of the season. They were sixth with three games to go, but lost 3-2 at Hartlepool, drew 1-1 at home to Bournemouth and then 1-1 at Bradford. They finished seventh, two points behind Swansea City in sixth and faced another season in League One.

FACT 88
2007
THROWING PROMOTION AWAY

Nottingham Forest condemned themselves to a third season in League One in 2006-07, falling out of the automatic promotion places and then blowing a two goal first leg lead in the play-offs.

Colin Calderwood was appointed as manager and Forest won their first four games. They were second in the table at the turn of the year, but lost 5-0 on New Year's Day at Oldham, who went above them in the table. Forest eventually finished fourth.

Forest won the first leg of their play-off semi-final 2-0 against Yeovil at Huish Park. At the City Ground on 18th May, Forest looked to be heading to Wembley with ten minutes remaining and the score 1-1. However, with eight minutes left Jean Paul Kalala's shot bounced off the post, hit Forest's Alan Wright on the leg and bobbled into the net. Five minutes later Marcus Stewart's header took the tie into extra time.

Forest were then dealt another blow when David Prutton was sent off. Early in extra time Yeovil went 4-1 ahead but Gary Holt brought it back level a minute later. In the second period, Wright suffered an injury effectively reducing Forest to nine men as all substitutes had been used. Arron Davies then made it 5-2, ending Forest's promotion hopes.

FACT 89

2007
BRIAN CLOUGH
TROPHY

In 2007 the Brian Clough Trophy was inaugurated, to be contested whenever Nottingham Forest and Derby County, the two clubs where he had most success, met each other.

The idea of the trophy came about in early 2007 after discussion between officials of both clubs, Brian's widow Barbara and son Nigel. The Brian Clough Memorial Fund was also involved, with revenue raised from the first game at Pride Park on 31st July going to good causes in the East Midlands.

Derby beat Forest 2-0 in that game watched by a crowd of 25,159. There was a moment of solidarity between the two sets of rival fans however when the whole stadium rose to sing "Stand up for Brian Clough."

In 2007-08 Forest were promoted from League One, and Derby relegated from the Premier League. Since then both sides have remained in the Championship and the two sides have competed for the trophy at least twice a season.

As of the end of 2019-20 the trophy, which is a silver cup over 100 years old, has been contested 28 times. 24 of these were in the league, two FA Cup, one League Cup and also the original game. It has changed hands nine times, with Forest being the holders as of summer 2020, regaining it in a 3-0 League Cup win on 27th August 2019.

FACT 90

2007
A FREE GOAL

Forest were leading Leicester City 1-0 in a League Cup tie on 28th August 2007 that was abandoned at half time due to the opposition's Clive Clarke suffering a cardiac arrest. In the replayed game, Leicester sportingly allowed Forest to score from the kick-off.

When the sides met again on 18th September, Leicester's players stood aside to allow Forest keeper Paul Smith to score from the kick-off. The goal was timed at 23 seconds and restored Forest's advantage from the first game.

Despite being handed this advantage Forest failed to make the most of it. They were leading 2-1 with two minutes remaining but conceded an equaliser and went on to lose 3-2 in extra time. The main talking point however was Leicester's act of sporting goodwill, the intentions of which Forest were made aware of twenty minutes before kick-off.

Forest boss Colin Calderwood said of the gesture "Leicester felt it was the correct thing to do and I must admit it took us back a little bit to start with. But it was an honourable gesture and I would like to think that football in general has come out of the game as the winner. I think the crowd took it in the spirit it was intended."

FACT 91
2008
PROMOTED ON
DRAMATIC LAST DAY

Forest finally escaped League One on a dramatic last day of the 2007-08 season, when they leapfrogged Doncaster Rovers to claim the second automatic promotion spot.

Amongst the five close season arrivals was Arron Davies, whose double for Yeovil at the City Ground in the play-offs condemned Forest to a third season in League One.

After a poor start, three successive wins in September got things going and Forest steadily climbed the table, reaching top spot by Christmas. However, they dropped out of the top two and looked destined for the play-offs.

Five wins from six in April then gave them an outside chance of going up automatically on the final day. Ironically, Forest were at home to Yeovil, who caused so much heartbreak a year earlier. They needed to win and hope Doncaster failed to collect three points in their game at Cheltenham.

At half time Forest led 3-1 and Doncaster trailed 1-0. It remained that way for the first thirty minutes of the second half but Yeovil pulled a goal back and Doncaster equalised around the same time.

With five minutes left Forest fans were buoyed by the news that Cheltenham had regained the lead. They held on for victory and there were joyous scenes at the end as Forest secured their return to the Championship.

FACT 92
2009 ESCAPING THE DROP

Forest looked set for a return to League One in 2008-09. However, the appointment of Billy Davies as manager turned things around and they beat the drop by going their last six games unbeaten.

Colin Calderwood made a number of changes to the squad that had secured promotion. The highest profile new arrival was Welsh international striker Robert Earnshaw, who arrived for £2.65 million from Derby County. It was a bold move given he had endured a torrid time with the Rams, scoring just once as they were relegated from the Premier League.

Forest struggled and just one win in their opening thirteen games left them bottom of the table. Calderwood was sacked after a 4-2 home defeat to Doncaster Rovers on Boxing Day. Caretaker manager John Pemberton oversaw a 3-2 win at Norwich, where Earnshaw scored a later winner. Billy Davies was then appointed and won his three games in charge to lift Forest out of the drop zone.

Three successive defeats in March saw Forest drop back into the bottom three with six games left. However, they hauled themselves out of it and a 1-1 draw at Blackpool in their penultimate game, coupled with Barnsley and Norwich dropping points, ensured survival. The signing of Earnshaw paid off as he finished top scorer with seventeen goals.

FACT 93
2010 PLAY-OFF DEFEAT

Forest continued their improvement under Billy Davies in 2009-10, finishing third in the table but missing out on promotion in the play-offs.

Forest won only one of their first eight games, but a 1-0 win at Plymouth Argyle on 25th September 2009 was the start of a five-game winning sequence that lifted them into the top half of the table.

Although the next four games were drawn, Forest remained unbeaten until the end of January. This was a total of nineteen matches and took them into second place. From February onwards Forest's away form let them down, losing seven in succession. However, their form at the City Ground, where they remained unbeaten since September, kept them comfortably in the play-off positions.

In the play-off semi-final Forest faced Blackpool. At Bloomfield Road, Chris Cohen gave them a 1-0 lead, but the home side came from behind to win 2-1.

At the City Ground Robert Earnshaw gave Forest an early lead and it remained 1-0 at half time. In a thrilling second half Blackpool hit back but Earnshaw restored Forest's advantage on the night. However, they were stunned when Blackpool scored three times in seven minutes and it finished 4-3 on the night, 5-3 on aggregate.

FACT 94

2011
SECOND SUCCESSIVE
PLAY-OFF DEFEAT

In 2010-11 Nottingham Forest missed out on promotion via the play-offs for a second successive season.

Unlike in 2009-10, Forest's participation in the play-offs was by no means certain. Their form was erratic throughout the season which started off with seven draws in their first eleven games, leaving them in fifteenth.

Forest slowly climbed the table and six straight wins after New Year lifted them into second place. They then won just one game from twelve, falling down to eighth. By winning their last four games, Forest climbed back into the play-off positions and finished the regular season in sixth.

The first leg of the play-off semi-final against Swansea was at the City Ground. Swansea were reduced to ten men after just two minutes when Neil Taylor was sent off, but Forest couldn't capitalise, and it finished 0-0.

At the Liberty Stadium on 16th May, Forest trailed 2-0 at half time. With ten minutes remaining Robert Earnshaw pulled a goal back. There was then agony in injury time when Earnshaw hit the post and with Lee Camp out of his goal, Swansea broke away and scored a third. Billy Davies was sacked in the close season and Forest have not appeared in the play-offs since.

FACT 95
2011
A LEAGUE CUP
DERBY

The first Nottingham derby of the 21st Century took place on 9th August 2011. After a thrilling 3-3 draw in the first round of the League Cup, Forest progressed on penalties.

This was the second time Forest had played Notts County in the country's second cup competition. The other was in 1977-78 when Forest won 4-0.

Michael Edwards opened the scoring for County in the sixteenth minute but Lewis McGugan equalised after half an hour. In the second half, Robert Findley gave Forest a 56th minute lead but Craig Westcarr forced extra time with a quarter of an hour to go.

County's Lee Hughes scored midway through the first period of extra time and looked to have secured their first victory at the City Ground since 1982. However, in stoppage time, Westley Morgan's long-range effort took the game to penalties.

Forest's Jonathan Greening hit the post with the first kick but after five each it was 3-3. In sudden death Luke Chambers converted his kick before County's Neal Bishop missed, sending Forest into the next round.

Despite the rarity of the fixture, the attendance of 21,605 was less than had watched Forest's Championship fixture against Barnsley three days earlier. This was a clear indication that Forest fans see Derby as more serious rivals than their neighbours from across the River Trent.

FACT 96

2013
OUT OF THE PLAY-OFFS
IN INJURY TIME

On the last day of the 2012-13 season Nottingham Forest lost at home to Leicester City for the first time in forty years. In a dramatic match, Forest conceded in injury time meaning Leicester moved above them into the play-off positions.

In February Billy Davies was appointed as Forest manager for the second time, with them in eleventh place. A run of six straight victories took them into the play-off places, but five games without a win saw a drop to eighth with three remaining.

On the final day of the season Forest were at home to Leicester, knowing they could make it into the play-offs providing they bettered Bolton's result against Blackpool. Leicester also knew that if Bolton slipped up they could sneak into the play-offs with victory.

Simon Cox gave Forest the perfect start when he scored in the third minute. Leicester struck back to lead 2-1 at half time, but Matty James equalised soon after the break. With Bolton only drawing, Forest poured forward in search of a winner. They were then caught on the break as Anthony Knockeart scored in injury time to secure the Foxes first win at Forest since 1972 and a play-off spot.

FACT 97

2015
STUART PEARCE SACKED

Although a legend as a player with Nottingham Forest, Stuart Pearce's return as manager was not a happy one. He was sacked on 1st February 2015 after just seven months in charge.

In his twelve years as a player at Forest between 1985 and 1997, Pearce made over 400 league appearances, most of them as captain. He was an uncompromising but fair left back, whose strong shot made him a dead ball specialist.

During his time at Forest Pearce played 76 times for England, making him the club's most capped player. In his last season, 1996-97, he was caretaker player-manager for two months in between the axing of Frank Clark and appointment of Dave Bassett.

After leaving the City Ground Pearce played on for five more seasons, his last game coming just three days before his fortieth birthday. He then managed Manchester City, England Under 21's and the Great Britain side in the 2012 Olympics.

Pearce was appointed as Forest manager in the summer of 2014. The season started well and Forest were second after ten games. However, after Christmas they lost five from six, as well as suffering an embarrassing FA Cup defeat at Rochdale. Pearce was sacked with the club in twelfth place and replaced by Dougie Freedman.

FACT 98

2017
STAYING UP AND
A NEW BEGINNING

Nottingham Forest endured a torrid season in 2016-17, only avoiding relegation on goal difference. After the season ended the club came into new ownership and the hope of a brighter future.

Before the season had begun Forest were in trouble with the local council, who reduced the ground capacity by 20% due to problems with the safety certificate. This issue was resolved by the time of the second home game against Wigan, which Forest won 4-3. This made it two wins and two defeats from the opening four fixtures.

Forest had a dreadful autumn, winning just once in eleven games during September and October. Philippe Montanier was sacked in January and Gary Brazil filled in on a caretaker basis for two months before Mark Warburton was appointed.

Despite not being in the relegation zone all season, Forest still needed a win on the last day to be sure of staying up and even then it was close. They beat Ipswich 3-0 at the City Ground and were thankful that Blackburn could only win 3-1 at Brentford. It meant Forest had avoided relegation thanks to their goal difference of minus ten, compared to Blackburn's minus twelve.

Ten days after the season ended, a consortium led by Greek businessman Evangelos Marinakis bought the club, promising to do all he could to restore success.

FACT 99
2018 NOTTINGHAM FOREST'S RECORD SIGNING

In the summer of 2018 Nottingham Forest broke their transfer record, paying £13.2 million for Portuguese midfielder Joao Carvalho.

Carvalho, a 21-year-old attacking midfielder, was signed from Benfica where he mainly played in their reserve side. He did however make a Champions League appearance and also played fifteen games in the Portuguese top-flight whilst on loan at Vitoria Setubal in 2016-17.

The £13.2 million fee was more than double Forest's previous transfer record and a clear statement of intent by owner Evangelos Marinakas. It showed that he wanted to make a push for the Premiership after finishing in the bottom half of the Championship for four seasons running.

Carvalho flourished in the first half of 2018-19, developing an excellent understanding with Lewis Grabban. However, when manager Aitor Karanka left the club by mutual consent in January 2019 his replacement Martin O'Neill preferred a more physical approach and Carvalho was used less frequently.

O'Neill was sacked in June 2019 after failing to make the play-offs but a pre-season injury impacted on Carvalho's ability to impress new manager Sabri Lamouchi. He was in and out of the side in 2019-20, making 23 appearances under a manager whose preference was for holding midfielders.

FACT 100
2020 POST PANDEMIC PAIN

Nottingham Forest looked certain to reach the play-offs in 2019-20, a season that was disrupted by the COVID-19 pandemic. However, when the Championship resumed in June, they ended up missing out on goal difference.

Forest lost 3-0 at home to Millwall on 6th March, a result that seriously dented their hopes of going up automatically. However, they were six points ahead of seventh place with nine games to go. The following week, elite football in England was suspended as the COVID-19 pandemic worsened.

When it was safe to resume playing behind closed doors in June, Forest picked up seven points from the first nine available. However, at Derby on 4th July Forest conceded a last-minute equaliser. They still looked certainties for the play-offs but a defeat at home to Fulham followed by draws with Preston and Swansea saw the gap close.

In their penultimate game against Barnsley, Forest looked to have secured a play-off spot, only for the home side to score an injury time winner.

A point at home to Stoke on the final day would still be enough, but Forest collapsed in the second half and lost 4-1. Swansea won by the same score line at Reading and Forest missed out on goal difference, dropping out of the play-off positions for the first time since December.

The 100 Facts Series

Arsenal, *Steve Horton*	978-1-908724-09-0
Aston Villa, *Steve Horton*	978-1-908724-98-4
Celtic, *Steve Horton*	978-1-908724-10-6
Chelsea, *Kristian Downer*	978-1-908724-11-3
Everton, *Bob Sharp*	978-1-908724-12-0
Hearts, *Steve Horton*	978-1-912782-48-2
Leeds, *Steve Horton*	978-1-908724-94-6
Leicester City, *Steve Horton*	978-1-912782-47-5
Liverpool, *Steve Horton*	978-1-908724-13-7
Manchester City, *Steve Horton*	978-1-908724-14-4
Manchester United, *Iain McCartney*	978-1-908724-15-1
Newcastle United, *Steve Horton*	978-1-908724-16-8
Norwich City, *Steve Horton*	978-1-908724-99-1
Nottingham Forest, *Steve Horton*	978-1-912782-46-8
Rangers, *David Clayton*	978-1-908724-17-5
Sheffield United, *Steve Horton*	978-1-912782-45-1
Tottenham Hotspur, *Steve Horton*	978-1-908724-18-2
West Ham, *Steve Horton*	978-1-908724-80-9

Player Autographs

Player Autographs

Player Autographs

Player Autographs

Player Autographs